The Pursuit of Pleasure

GOD: the ultimate delight

William L. Smith

malcolm down
PUBLISHING

Copyright © 2017 William L. Smith

21 20 19 18 17   7 6 5 4 3 2 1

First published 2017 by Malcolm Down Publishing Ltd.
www.malcolmdown.co.uk

The right of William L. Smith to be identified as the author of this work has been asserted by him in accordance with the Copyright, Designs and Patents Act 1988.

All rights reserved. No part of this publication may be reproduced, stored in a retrieval system, or transmitted in any other form or by any means, electronic, mechanical, photocopying, recording or otherwise, without the prior permission of the publisher.

British Library Cataloguing in Publication Data
A catalogue record for this book is available from the British Library.

ISBN 978-1-910786-68-0

Unless otherwise indicated, Scripture quotations taken from The Holy Bible, New International Version (Anglicised edition) Copyright ©1979, 1984, 2011 by Biblica (formerly International Bible Society). Used by permission of Hodder & Stoughton Publishers, an Hachette UK company. All rights reserved. 'NIV' is a registered trademark of Biblica (formerly International Bible Society). UK trademark number 1448790.

Scripture quotations marked TPT are taken from Song of Songs: *Divine Romance* and The Psalms: *Poetry on Fire*, The Passion Translation copyright 2014, 2015. Used by permission of Broadstreet Publishing Group, LLC, Racine, Wisconsin, USA. All rights reserved. www.thepassiontranslation.com.

Scripture taken from the One New Man Bible, copyright 2011 William J. Morford. Used by permission of True Potential Publishing, Inc.

Scripture taken from THE MESSAGE, copyright 1993, 1994, 1995, 1996, 2000, 2001, 2002. Used by permission of NavPress Publishing Group

Cover design by Esther Kotecha

Printed in the UK

Contents

Dedication		04
Acknowledgements		05
Endorsements		06
Introduction		07
Chapter 1	In the Beginning	11
Chapter 2	God's Pleasure	21
Chapter 3	Giving God's People Pleasure	39
Chapter 4	Pressure and Pleasure	55
Chapter 5	Pleasure in One Another	77
Chapter 6	Displeasure	89
Chapter 7	Pleasure in the Father	107
Chapter 8	Treasure, Price and Value	125
Chapter 9	Ecclesiastes	141
Chapter 10	The Song of Songs	143
Chapter 11	The Song of Songs 2	177
Chapter 12	Do You Love Me More Than These?	189

Dedication

I would like to dedicate this book to all the lovers and followers of Jesus who long for His glory to be seen in the Church. I pray these pages may add something to the conversation.

Acknowledgements

To Abba God, the Delight of my life, I give You thanks for the privilege and opportunity to pen these pages. For the passion which You have enabled to flow into words. May they bring glory to Your beautiful name.

To Susanna, my wife, my support, my encourager and my most precious friend. Thank you for all that you have been as we have walked this path together. Your input has been invaluable. I love you so much.

To my children and grandchildren, may these pages excite a greater desire for God.

To my dear friends from Lionhunt whose love and laughter over these past years has been such a strength. I love you dearly.

To Charlie Coombes, thanks for allowing me to use some thoughts from your heart.

To Teresa White, thank you for your initial reading and thoughts on my manuscript. And especially for allowing me to show something of your passion for your beloved Papa. You are dear and precious to us both.

Endorsements

'One of the greatest themes of the Bible is the pleasure of God. We were made to enjoy His pleasure and to bring Him pleasure. In exploring this theme, Bill has done us a great service. He has shown us how to bring joy to the Lover of our souls and, in the process, to delight in the passionate love of the Living God. What could be more pleasurable than that?'
Dr Mark Stibbe
Best-selling, award-winning author
CEO of Kingdom Writing Solutions

'William Smith really brings this whole subject of God's pleasure verses our pleasure to the forefront of our minds as we pursue God in this season of transformation. I believe this book will pinpoint the degree of pleasure we have for the kingdom and how that will manifest through our worship life, prayer life and relationship we have with him. It will also help us discover the priorities of what type of pleasure is important and bring us to a sobering conviction of what type of pleasure we have allowed into our relationships that have affected us not to understand and enjoy God's good pleasure.

I would recommend both leaders and the Body of Christ to read this as it will help evaluate the type of relationship we have with the Lord and His kingdom, and how we don't have to live around the distorted version that the world wants us to embrace; get to know the true nature of God and His good pleasure for your life.'
Dr David McDonald
North Charleston Apostolic Center International

Introduction

Pleasure – one of humanity's basic and strongest forces. We all strive for pleasure all the time. The feelings of enjoyment, satisfaction and meaning are extremely strong and drive us to achieve them. Basically, we do what we do for the sake of pleasure. I know this is the basic tenet of hedonism, but I cannot see why it should be militated against simply because hedonism suggests the fulfilment of sensual appetites as paramount. 'If it feels good, do it' is a contemporary expression which denotes this. My intention in the following pages is to demonstrate that sensual appetites are not exclusive in the understanding of pleasure.

There are those who, as followers of the ancient Epicureans, value intellectual and social pleasures much more than the sensual. Perhaps it is nothing other than a different expression of the sensual, since our feelings are stirred even as we attempt to evaluate a tricky topic. The search for intellectual satisfaction is equally as strong as the mere fleshly appetites. De Sade became famous, or should that be infamous, for promoting blatant sexual pleasures. This was often through forms which brought pain to others. Maybe the schoolyard bully fits within this remit, simply for the enjoyment of inflicting pain on another person. We are all familiar with the expression that 'hurt people, hurt people'. Even from a young age this can be demonstrated. We are all conscious of the enormous desires of our sexual drive and its felt need for fulfilment and satisfaction. But is that all it is? I believe it has needs that are found in meaningful relationships, not simply the sex act. Relationship is the heart of God. The heart that expresses its desire for relationship with us seen in the sacrifice of Jesus on our behalf.

De Sade's ideas have been further developed by Herbert Spencer who equated right and wrong with pleasure and pain. Thus pleasure can be seen in its ultimate sense as defining ethics, since what pleases us and gives us joy also benefits our survival. I am not convinced that idea can stand up to hard scrutiny. People get drunk for the pleasure of it, in their own minds, for instance. I cannot conceive of drunkenness being beneficial to our survival. Whereas the hedonist will claim that pleasure is the only intrinsic good. I wonder how good being in a drunken stupor proves to be.

What Freud called the 'pleasure principle' was the psychoanalytical concept describing people seeking pleasure and avoiding pain. The pleasure principle is a driven force, whose counterpart is the reality principle. This is when we choose to abstain from the gratification of a desire, even a cup of coffee for instance, when circumstantial reality prevents it.

However we may confront these philosophical ideas, we cannot deny our insatiable desire for pleasure, nor the extreme lengths some will go to in achieving it.

Given that we are created in the image and likeness of God (Genesis 1:26), it must be that God desires pleasure. Since God is complete in every way, lacking nothing, His expressions of desire towards us must be to draw humanity into His pleasure. From this we have to acknowledge that since God is complete in every way, then He is equally pleasure, even as He is love, just, holy and faithful.

In these pages I am looking at and seeking to construct a framework in which God is recognised and enjoyed as the

Introduction

Ultimate Delight of the believer, and how that impacts upon us. The Westminster Catechism states that the chief end of man is to worship God and enjoy Him forever.

Little children early in life develop a very strong pleasure aspect. They quickly learn what makes them squeal with delight, as well as what causes them to cry. Their pleasure is so often found in very simple experiences. As we grow older we demand more sophisticated means of pleasure and make use of our abilities to achieve it. But Jesus calls us to be as little children in matters pertaining to Him and His kingdom. I pray we may find our pleasure in simply loving God with all our heart, soul, mind and strength.

This is the purpose of this book.

Chapter 1
In The Beginning

The Bible begins with these dramatic words 'In the beginning God'. As Christians, we believe that God is the source of all that is. In Him was the thought, the idea, the developed plan, and the fulfilment of that, so that all that is has issued from Him.

'By faith we understand that the universe was formed at God's command, so that what is seen was not made out of what was visible' (Hebrews 11:3).

The world we see is marvellous. A magnificent delight to the senses, and why not? Since we read 'God saw all that he had made, and it was very good' (Genesis 1:31). This delight-filled wonder has come from the being of God. Truly He is a delightful, wonderful God.

'Great and marvellous are Your deeds, Lord God Almighty' (Revelation 15:3).

When we read in Scripture of God's wonderful, or wondrous deeds, it speaks of that which excites admiration, and produces something exceedingly pleasing. This is the import of the original Hebrew. I commend to you a fresh reading of the magnificent Psalm 104, the Creation Psalm. Our great Creator God creates that which is magnificently, gloriously delightful. He is the God 'who alone does marvellous deeds' (Psalm 72:18) This tells me that God is the only One who does that which is wonderful, and also that He is the One who only does wonderful things. There is no enabling, no power, apart from God, to do that which is marvellous. As we turn to look at ourselves, the crown of His creation, are you, again, confronted with the God who elicits praise? 'I am fearfully and wonderfully made; your works are wonderful' (Psalm 139:14). As I learn of our making and the amazing intricacies of the human frame and being, I am awestruck and filled with wonder. Having been present at the birth of most of my children (one delivery was complicated. I had to wait outside), I am still awed at the sight and incredible wonder of a new-born child. The contemptible idea that we 'just happened' without any plan or purpose staggers me.

We worship the God of great wonders who leaves me staggered by His marvellous, delightful creative works. Who is not struck by the simple beauty of a flower? A flower, which upon closer inspection is found to be constructed of the most delicate, fragile parts, beautifully and marvellously blended into a delight-inducing whole. We see this replicated throughout the natural world. At every turn, amazing colours, intricate physical detail and a plethora of design on display to leave us gasping in wonder and delight. This is God. The Creator of great wonders. The God who incites us to such heights of pleasure in His handiwork.

Through the prophet He asks, 'To whom will you compare me? … Lift up your eyes … to the heavens: who created all these?' (Isaiah 40:25–26). Who or what can compare with our glorious heavenly Father God? Where is the one who can even stand in the shadow of Almighty God as a contender for His throne? There is no God but God. 'Before me no god was formed, nor will there be one after me. I, even I, am the LORD, and apart from me there is no saviour' (Isaiah 43:10–11). Again I am dumbfounded that people believe it all just happened by accident, without thought or purpose. How many of us find pleasure walking in the countryside? Across the moors or mountains? Along the banks of a river, or a clifftop staring out to sea? Through the woods or along the seashore? All this a blind chance accident?

God speaks of His glorious splendour, exciting our spirits to wonder and awe, that bring us to worship. He does not need our worship. He was utterly complete and content in Himself, lacking nothing, before He ever spoke into the void and brought life and order to His creations. Yet, because He is God, He has to create. Worship changes us. It doesn't change God. It can stimulate in us an awareness of His majestic glory. This causes me to realise just how small and petty we are before Him. Yet He exalts us to His throne in Jesus and pours His glory upon and into us. As we worship we become like Him. Is the worship of our whole being, devoted to Him constantly, in everything, the greatest and deepest delight and joy? Who or what can compare?

Hear His thundering declaration, and marvel. 'It is I who made the earth and created mankind on it. My own hands stretched out the heavens; I marshalled their starry hosts' (Isaiah 45:12). Wow, are you not struck dumb by the greatness, the sheer power and creative wonders of our God? Only to find a voice which must praise Him… A voice which must adore and speak of His mighty acts and all the wonders of His Being! The heavens declare the glory of God. The skies proclaim the works of His hands. So much that 'since the creation of the world God's invisible qualities – his eternal power and divine nature, have been clearly seen' (Romans 1:20). The psalmist emphasised this theme centuries before Paul's statement. 'The heavens declare the glory of God; the skies proclaim the work of his hands. Day after day they pour forth speech; night after night they display knowledge. There is no speech or language where their voice is not heard. Their voice goes out into all the earth, their words to the ends of the world' (Psalm 19:1–4, NIV 1984). Everywhere humanity lives, God's greatness is expressed through His masterful creation. This explains to us the volumes and anthems of creation's voice bringing consciousness to all humanity that God is the Creator. Whatever language, wherever it is spoken, creation declares, more than that, it thunders out, the inescapable truth, leaving all people everywhere without excuse, that all this did not just happen. Creation proclaims the intricate, glorious, love- filled handiwork of the One and Only True and Living God, the Creator of all that is, seen and unseen. Closing our hearts as well as our eyes to this inescapable glorious truth brings us pain and sorrow. Pain and sorrow cause us to seek after pleasure with greater purpose and passion. Paul tells us that so much of humankind has deliberately closed its eyes to God's glory, thereby suppressing His truth and turning to idolatry by making its own gods. Its own means of finding pleasure and satisfaction. This is seen in the worship of what God has made, rather than the worship of God the Maker. Such arrogant foolishness leads to all manner of perversity in the quest for fulfilment. This illustrates the consequences of turning from the Ultimate Pleasure to taste something that is toxic, though attractive to the senses, as the rest of Romans chapter 1 tells us.

Come with me into the most famous garden on earth. We read how God planted this garden, and filled it with wonderful life and beautiful trees and vegetation. Trees that were pleasing to the eye and good for food. Sounds idyllic, doesn't it? And so it was. Everything God made had His own stamp of approval on it. It was good. There could be nothing more 'good' than God's own 'good'. God's creation has already been seen as His magnificent, delightful, desirable craftsmanship. We could argue that this stunningly beautiful creation, an expression of His delight and character, became the architect of its own downfall. In chapter

3 of Genesis we read how the woman, when tempted, was so attracted by it. She saw that the fruit of the tree was good for food and pleasing to the eye, and also desirable for gaining wisdom, so she took some and ate it. I have always puzzled at the idea that they could have wanted more than the 'everything' that is perfect and satisfying that God offered them to enjoy. Then I acknowledge, for myself, how I, also, want more than this same everything of God, every time I give in to temptation, as if He is not enough.

The huge international space telescopes searching out the depths of space reveal things unseen by the naked eye, which are staggering in magnificence, and all from our one galaxy. One among millions. We inhabit one small spot among the amazing array of magnificent creation. I am one tiny speck of dust on this one tiny lump called earth. Yet God knows me, by name. He knows you by name. Where can I find another in whom such a boast can be made? I cannot. He is God alone. Glorious in majesty and power. Magnificent in splendour. Does not your heart reach out to Him as you grasp something of who He is? He excites such a response, since we are made for pleasure, His pleasure. Read afresh the opening words of Ephesians telling us it is all for His pleasure. It gives God pleasure to call us to Himself in salvation grace and love, making us His holy, blameless, chosen children.

Ecclesiastes tells us that 'He has made everything beautiful in its time. He has set eternity in the human heart' (3:10–11). Eternity set in our hearts. That searching for something deeper, that something beyond ourselves that we reach towards. That longing to know and be known. That desire to live forever in delight.

'You are worthy, our Lord and God, to receive glory and honour and power, for you created all things, and by your will [or for Your pleasure] they were created and have their being' (Revelation 4:11). God's will is God's pleasure. God's pleasure is God's will.

Somehow in the deep mysteries of God, He who is the absolute fullness of pleasure in Himself, derives pleasure from His creative brilliance and unsullied handiwork. Because He is creative, He creates. This is always pleasurable since pleasure is who He is. It must be the sheer joy of expressing Himself in Himself for Himself, such that this pleasure emanates.

Well, that is my effort at trying to get my head around it!

'I've done a good job there,' is His comment on His creation. Creation is an expression of His pleasure. The God of pleasure, in and for His own pleasure, creates this pleasure-ball called earth. Then He places His pleasure-created creatures on it. Beings who are created in pleasure and filled with desire for pleasure. How inevitable it is that God's kingdom is joy, in the Holy Spirit. The Spirit of God is the Spirit of joy.

The Garden of Eden, created especially for the pleasure and fulfilment of humanity, with delights beyond human comprehension, was spoiled by the sin of disobedience. The sin of doubting God. Because of that, this earth that fills us with wonder and joy is a shadow of the original. The original that is waiting to be restored. The most spectacular waterfall, or mountain peak; the most beautiful flower, or sweetest of creatures; the most stunning sunset, or fearful storm, is holding its breath, as it were, till the day that God's new creation children come into the fullness of who they really are, and we see everything made new. So much more spectacular than our wildest imaginings (see Romans 8:19–21).

Back to the garden. The woman, who is living in the middle of this amazing garden, is at peace in its tranquillity and thrilled by

In The Beginning

its never-ending beauty. Into this idyllic scene comes something that turns her innocence into what has become one of the most destructive forces in human experience. The pursuit of pleasure. Pleasure apart from God. Pleasure devoid of healthy parameters. Pleasure, all-consuming and never satisfied. Allowing temptation to take root in her heart, she turns her worship away from God. This single act creates a distortion of truth. God is Truth. Turning away from Him is turning away from Truth. That is how she is able to see in the fruit something it does not possess. It does not possess the power to fulfil, to satisfy, to make one wise. Yet she sees this deception as though true. Taking the fruit, she eats some, gives some to her husband, and both of them become slaves to desire. Desire that can only be satisfied in God, yet they have turned from Him. As for making them wise, wisdom would have been listening to what God said, not allowing themselves to be deceived – does anyone seriously believe that hiding behind a tree means God does not know where you are? God's call was to their hearts. He knew they had turned from Him. His question is asking, 'Where are you now that you have turned away from Me?' Answer: 'Hiding behind a tree, gripped by fear, despair and an emptiness that wasn't there before.' (They knew that they were naked, fully exposed.)

They have the whole garden in which to satiate every desire. God has withheld nothing from them, apart from this tree. 'How much is enough?' is the question once asked of the richest man in the world at that time. He answered, 'Just a little bit more.' Someone has said that being thankful makes what you have sufficient. Notice what it was that turns the woman's heart. It was something pleasing and desirable. She has seen something that was not recognised previously. It was something she found herself longing after. The accuser has 'messed with her head'. This has turned her heart. And the desire of delight has caught her attention. It is hard to grasp that God, in all His beauty, majesty and glory is daily walking in the garden with them yet something as trivial as a piece of fruit, which God has created, grabs their hearts. Yes, it is hard to understand, but every one of us knows, all too well, what they were experiencing.

It was disobedience that resulted in the actions which plunged the whole cosmos into the consequences of sin. But, can you see the part that pleasure played in this catastrophic event?

What captivated their hearts was the promise of unimaginable delight – 'you will be like God' (Genesis 3:5). They were already 'like God'. They were made in His image. They were living in the most wonderful communion with God; a relationship we can only try to imagine this side of heaven. The idea that pleasure brings us the good that we long to attain, is dealt a death blow by this catastrophic act of the pursuit of pleasure. Living in the greatest pleasure it is possible to experience was not enough. Deception turned the heads of our first parents, turning their hearts and minds from truth, plunging them, and all humanity, into a desperate darkness of deceit. In this deceit-drenched darkness we have all, ever since, been pursuing pleasure as a way back to that garden, and life.

How has it come about that for so many, God is seen as anything other than delightful? For some He is a severe, obscure figure. Someone to be appeased with the most stoic of lifestyles. For others, He is a slave master demanding more and greater demonstrations of allegiance and servitude. 'I must' seems to be the way to get to God, hopefully. There are those to whom God is so distant as to be unknowable, yet always sought after through acts of religious sacrifice and prohibition. Through hopefully acceptable offerings. How can such caricatures develop when

In The Beginning

Scripture tells us plainly that in His Presence is fullness of Joy and at His right hand there are eternal pleasures?

The pages of this book are dedicated to encouraging a greater awareness and pursuit of God as pleasure, as Ultimate Delight and most to be desired. This is not a pursuit just for those who are above failure and weakness. It is the pursuit of all, especially those who know their frailty, while longing for relationship with the Father. A relationship that satisfies and yields peace and joy. The psalmists put it this way:

'I said to the LORD, "You are my Lord; apart from you, I have no good thing"'; 'You have made known to me the path of life; you will fill me with joy in your presence, with eternal pleasures at your right hand' (Psalm 16:2,11).

'Taste and see that the LORD is good; blessed is the one who takes refuge in him' (Psalm 34:8).

'Satisfy us in the morning with your unfailing love' (Psalm 90:14).

All these words from the pen and hearts of men who have failed. Men who turned from the pursuit of God to taste the deceptive allures of their own flesh and pride.

'Let him kiss me with the kisses of his mouth – for your love is more delightful than wine' (Song of Songs 1:2).

- If you are able, why not press the pause button on your life for a few moments, and contemplate the wonders and pleasure of the natural world? Allow them to impact your heart, and give God thanks and praise.
- Remind yourself of why you love Him.

Chapter 2
God's Pleasure

We speak of God in human terms. It is the only language we have. In our attempts to know and understand Him, we use the words that make sense in our dealings with one another. That makes it a reasonable thing to ask the question, what gives God pleasure? Put another way, I ask, what makes God happy? Now, we are not delving into the reality that God is all-sufficient in and of Himself. He has no need for anything to be added to Him or to complete Him. What I am doing is using His revelation of Himself in Scripture, to more fully understand His nature and heart towards us. Therefore when I ask, what makes God happy? I am not suggesting, for one moment, that God is not eternally full of delight in Himself. But in relation to His created beings, He reveals Himself as One who takes delight in what He has made, and delight in His righteous purposes.

This is revealed in the following verses:

'For Zion's sake I will not keep silent, for Jerusalem's sake, I will not remain quiet, till her vindication shines out like the dawn, her salvation like a blazing torch. The nations will see your vindication, and all kings your glory; you will be called by a new name that the mouth of the LORD will bestow. You will be a crown of splendour in the LORD's hand ... No longer will they call you Deserted, or name your land Desolate. But you will be called Hephzibah [My delight is in her] and your land Beulah [married] ... As a young man marries a young woman, so will your Builder marry you; as a bridegroom rejoices over his bride, so will your God rejoice over you' (Isaiah 62:1–5).

'I will create Jerusalem to be a delight and its people a joy. I will rejoice over Jerusalem and take delight in my people' (Isaiah 65:18–19).

One thing these words reveal to us is that God takes pleasure in His people

We make God happy! As the psalmist sumptuously declares, 'The king is enthralled by your beauty; honour him, for he is your Lord' (Psalm 45:11, NIV 1984).

What is it that causes Almighty God to become so filled with delight in us? He has every tree, plant, cloud formation, galaxy, snowflake, butterfly, all to enjoy, and to delight in their beauty and awesome ability. Yet He has set His affection on us. He has destined us for the throne. We were made for relationship. A relationship of pleasure and delight. He can delight in a sunset. But a sunset cannot delight in God. We are destined for relationship. The Scriptures are saturated with this amazing, exciting truth.

'The LORD takes delight [pleasure] in his people' (Psalm 149:4).

'The LORD delights in those who fear [reverence, hold in awe] him' (Psalm 147:11).

'The vineyard of the LORD Almighty is the house of Israel, and the men of Judah are the garden of his delight' (Isaiah 5:7, NIV 1984).

It is an amazing reality that you and I give God pleasure. Who, me? Yes, you. Not because you are brilliant, or hard-working. Not because you are a worship leader, or preacher. Not because you pray six times a day, and fast every month. Not because you are young, or even much older. Simply because in His own will and wisdom, He chose for us to make Him happy. Paul expansively reiterates this truth when he states that God chose us before creation to be His beloved, adopted children. Simply because it gave the Father pleasure. (Ephesians 1).

So extravagant is this delight of God that He magnifies His delight in His people to the extent that the words used earlier: 'I will rejoice over Jerusalem and take delight in my people' actually speaks of God springing and leaping about with the sheer delight He finds in us. It is the Hebrew word *'Gul'* which carries this meaning. The same word is found in Zephaniah 3:17: 'The LORD your God is with you, he is mighty to save. He will take great delight in you, he will quiet you with his love, he will rejoice over you with singing' (NIV 1984). In all the sweetness and quiet assurance of these promises, we have a God of love who so delights in us that leaping and twirling around as He sings to us is the way He expresses His pleasure.

This is the import of this word *'Gul'*.

Beloved, you are amazingly precious to God. In His pleasure He made you that He may lavish His delight upon you and bring you to the delights of who He is.

Alongside His delight in who we are, He has pleasure in the rightness of our living.

He is 'pleased with integrity' (1 Chronicles 29:17). God was pleased for 'the sake of his righteousness to make his law great and glorious' (Isaiah 42:21). God has pleasure when righteous living happens. Why? I believe there are two reasons. Firstly, His kingdom is exemplified by righteousness. His holy and just ways are manifestations of His kingdom. It is His nature. Secondly, because righteousness keeps us from harm and pain. Walking in righteous integrity keeps us from the harmful and destructive results of pleasing ourselves.

During the time of Ezra and Nehemiah, the people had corrupted their God-given covenant ways. There is a specific situation in which some had married women who were foreigners. This was forbidden under Mosaic Law. This spoke of compromise, of welcoming idol worship into the assembly. Ezra speaks to them. 'Now make confession to the LORD, the God of your fathers, and do his will' Ezra 10:11, NIV 1984). The word 'will' also means 'pleasure'. The command is to do that which pleases God, what gives Him pleasure. His pleasure is the unadulterated worship of His people. This is a strange event as we view it from our sophisticated twenty-first century perspective. The point I want to bring out is that God's pleasure is in the obedience of His people. It pleases Him when we go right back to the beginning of things and deal with them according to His life-giving truth. David recognised this as he says 'You do not delight in sacrifice, or I would bring it; you do not take pleasure in burnt offerings. The sacrifices of God are a broken spirit; a broken and contrite heart, O God, you will not despise' (Psalm 51:16-17, NIV 1984). This was following his adulterous relationship with Bathsheba. Getting to the root of our waywardness and bringing it to the cross is what pleases God. That is what the cross is about. It is what the cross was for. Our repentance releases His grace to us.

The Father has pleasure in the outworking of His purposes

Jesus tells His disciples that God is pleased to give them His kingdom. So great is His desire for this that Isaiah startlingly declares that 'it was the LORD's will [it pleased Him] to crush him and cause him to suffer, and though the LORD makes his life an offering for sin, he will see his offspring and prolong his days, and the will [pleasure] of the LORD will prosper in his hand'

(Isaiah 53:10). This is amplified in Ephesians where Paul states that God has delight in bringing us into sonship (see Ephesians 1:2–6). He is delighted to adopt us as His children. So great is His delight in this that for Jesus, the excruciating embrace of all that the cross entailed was to Him 'the joy ... set before him' (Hebrews 12:2). This is such a deep mystery, plunging into the depths of God's heart. So great is the love of God that He has prepared a Bride for Himself, the reward of His suffering, you and me. This staggering, mind-blowing purpose was established in eternity past. So firmly set are God's purposes that He declares, 'My purpose will stand, and I will do all that I please' (Isaiah 46:10). This is more than simply being pleased. The weight of the language in Hebrew speaks of delight. God has delight in the unfolding and fulfilling of His purposes.

The amazing gift to us of His kingdom; the promises of accomplishing in, and through, us, all that He has determined; the security of His everlasting promises, all have their birth in His delight. All this faithful, compassionate, covenant love comes from the delight of His heart.

This is why He whoops and twirls, and jumps about with joyful singing, because of the delight He finds in you and me. I exaggerate not.

We also read how God has purposed to unite us all in one Body

This is vividly illustrated in Corinthians where Paul uses the imagery of a human body as the example of the collective body of believers. He states that 'God has arranged the parts in the body, every one of them, just as he wanted them to be [or as it pleased Him]' (1 Corinthians 12:18, NIV 1984). Each of us is an individual, essential part of this one Body of Christ. In this we function according to the 'part' we are, for the good of the

The Pursuit of Pleasure

whole, and in cooperation with the whole. No part of a human body operates independently. My left arm does not go off and make coffee while my right arm, and the rest of me, is sitting writing this. All of me has to leave the desk and go to the kitchen to make coffee.

Psalm 133 illustrates the Father's joy in unity. We are without excuse for every expression of division, disunity, separation, isolation, individualism and denominationalism. All of these are contrary to the Father's heart, I believe. God was pleased to have all the fullness of God inhabit Jesus on earth. God has never divided Himself up. He is always all that He is. And, contrary to most of Christian belief, I do not believe He left Jesus alone when He hung on the cross. God cannot separate Himself up. I dare to suggest that when Jesus spoke out those words on the cross 'My God, my God, why have you forsaken me?' He was preaching to the crowd the truth of who He was and is. Psalm 22 is a prophetic Messianic poem. It begins with dereliction and ends in triumph. It was an unfolding of what the people were witnessing. The masses knew their Scriptures. At the sound of those words most would have rehearsed the rest of the psalm. They lived in a culture which learned by heart the Scriptures. They had this oral tradition, so Jesus' words were familiar and poignant to their senses.

We are in Christ Jesus, Jesus is in us. All the unity of God lives in us. How can we live in separation? How did we manage to create so many Christian ghettos? One Body in Him is the prayer of Jesus in John chapter 17. It is the work of the Holy Spirit, who has baptised us into one Body. This is the pleasure of God. It is His purpose. We must, as the greatest priority of the whole Church, fix our attention on becoming what Jesus has already established through His death and resurrection.

God's Pleasure

The presentation of the good news of Jesus is also the Father's pleasure

We read that 'God was pleased through the foolishness of what was preached to save those who believe' (1 Corinthians 1:21). When Paul was telling his own salvation story, he said that God was pleased to reveal Jesus in him, so that he could preach Jesus to others (see Galatians 1:15–16). Every time we witness to Jesus, the Father is thrilled. And why not, since the gospel is still God's power for salvation to everyone who will believe. Even in the twenty-first century! It is God's joy that the good news is the means of bringing people to a living faith in Him. As Romans tells us, people cannot call on the One in whom they have never believed. And they cannot believe unless someone tells them. Also no one can tell them unless they are sent by God to tell them. As it says, 'How beautiful are the feet of those who bring good news!' (Romans 10:15). When we read in Acts of the Holy Spirit telling the Church to separate Paul and Barnabas to travel the Mediterranean nations preaching the gospel, and when we read of Jesus telling His disciples that when filled with Holy Spirit, they will witness to Him throughout the whole world, we are reading of a God who is not contriving to win a game of chess by thinking up new moves to outwit His opponent. Not at all. It has always been God's pleasure to bring us into cooperation with Him in seeing His kingdom come on earth as it is in heaven.

The end product is God's joy, His great pleasure and gladness in presenting us faultless and full of joy before His glorious Presence. We were destined for the throne from eternity past. This is why Paul prays 'that our God may count you worthy of his calling, and that by his power he may fulfil every good purpose of yours and every act prompted by your faith. We pray this so that the name of our Lord Jesus may be glorified in you, and you

The Pursuit of Pleasure

in him, according to the grace of our God and the Lord Jesus Christ' (2 Thessalonians 1:11–12, NIV 1984).

There is so much that flows from God's pleasure that returns, bringing pleasure to Him. Since all that is comes out of His pleasure, then, inevitably, everything that nature offers returns pleasure to God. All that is righteous in us, returns pleasure to God. So, with this in mind, we turn to this facet of this choicest jewel of pleasure.

The first hint we find in Scripture of giving pleasure to God is in the story of Cain and Abel.

Both of them bring an offering to God. Both brought an offering of the fruit of their labours. We read that God looked with favour on Abel's gift but not on Cain's gift. In the story we read that God told Cain why his gift was not acceptable and pleasing to Him: 'if you do not do what is right, sin is crouching at your door' (Genesis 4:7). The heart of Abel was pleasing to God and that is why his gift was acceptable. This touches on the core of every dealing God has with people. 'The matter of the heart, is the heart of the matter.' Everything always returns to the heart. It is not so much the gift we bring to God that pleases Him, but the heart with which we offer it. He is not pleased with a reluctant giver. He delights in an extravagant one. Remember the poor widow whom Jesus witnessed bringing a tiny offering to the synagogue? Her penny was worth more in God's sight than the wallet full of money others gave, for God looked at her heart, and it pleased Him. Everything always returns to the condition and attitude of our heart. Enoch was a man who was noted for his walk with God. He lived a very long life, and every day was lived in fellowship with God. Enoch did not die, for God took Him home with Him one day while they walked together. It is recorded that 'he was commended as one who pleased God. And

God's Pleasure

without faith it is impossible to please God' (Hebrews 11:5-6). The emphasis in the text here is on how well Enoch pleased God. There is such a depth of pleasure coming to God from this constant, faithful man.

It is everywhere in Scripture how God is pleased by the righteousness of His children. To the Thessalonian believers Paul speaks of their way of life pleasing God. Beyond that, he urges them to even greater devotion of heart and life. He assures them of God's pleasing will for them to be made more like Jesus (1 Thessalonians 4:1-3a). Who among us does not want to become more like Jesus?

Paul speaks of his own commitment to pleasing God instead of pleasing men. This can prove a great challenge to leaders and people of influence within the Church. We all want to be liked, to be popular. We don't easily volunteer to be unpopular by speaking truth to those who would rather not hear it.

Solomon stands out during the early days of his reign when his integrity was still intact. It was the witness of his heart when God said to him, 'Ask for whatever you want me to give you.'

What an open chequebook that is! Fame, fortune, popularity, the devotion of beautiful women, victory over his enemies, to rule the world... All this is offered to him. What do we see Solomon do? He bares his soul to God, confessing his immaturity to govern, and asks God for the wisdom he needs to govern with integrity and wisdom. God was so pleased with Solomon because of the selflessness of his request. And God blessed him with an abundance of the things he had not asked for. You read the story in 1 Kings chapter 3. In Proverbs we see testimony to the life of Solomon when we read, 'When a man's ways are pleasing to the LORD, he makes even his enemies live at peace with him' (Proverbs 16:7, NIV 1984). Peace with his neighbours was a notable aspect of Solomon's reign.

Jesus gives us His peace. Peace which is so much more than the lack of hostilities that the world recognises as peace. His is a peace which is full of assurance and security. We have the assurance of knowing that He is always working for our good in whatever we face. We have the security of knowing that His hold on us is so much stronger than our hold on Him. So strong that nothing can snatch us from His hand. Nothing can undermine His love and commitment to us. This is the reality of being joined in faith to the God of all creation. It is the reality of the seal of the Holy Spirit, the guarantee of our eternal inheritance, as Ephesians tells us. I believe it is also the security and peace of understanding that it is not our righteousness that holds us in His love, but it is His love that holds us secure, whatever is happening in our life. He knows our frailties. He is equally aware of our failings, and we are loved passionately, purposefully and completely, despite that. What a place of pleasure in which our hearts and minds can rest.

Walking in joyful, righteous obedience pleases the Father and matures in us the good things of kingdom sonship. Micah helps us to see what this entails: 'With what shall I come before the LORD and bow down before the exalted God? Shall I come before him with burnt offerings, with calves a year old? Will the LORD be pleased with thousands of rams, and with ten thousand rivers of oil? Shall I offer my firstborn for my transgression, the fruit of my body for the sin of my soul? He has shown you, O mortal, what is good. And what does the LORD require of you? To act justly and to love mercy and to walk humbly before your God' (Micah 6:6–8).

No amount of religious observance can take the place of a life of obedience. God doesn't count our attendance at various Christian meetings and events as much as He looks into our hearts to see if

God's Pleasure

devotion or duty is the reason. To see if service or self-satisfaction is our motive. I believe God is always looking for a heart and a life in holy cooperation in the ways of His kingdom. Malachi emphasises this as he speaks of God as a refiner and purifier. To purify His people so that they bring righteous offerings before His throne, the offerings that God accepts (see Malachi 3:2-4). We have confidence in Jesus, whose blood cleanses us from sin, that we can come boldly to the throne, finding the grace we need to help us in our walk. If you are like me, you are conscious of the struggles and failures; the weakness and unkept promises. But we have a Father who sees beyond what we see and feel, as He sees us complete in Jesus.

Through Jesus, therefore, let us continually offer to God a sacrifice of praise. The fruit of lips that confess His name. 'And do not forget to do good and to share with others, for with such sacrifices God is pleased' (Hebrews 13:16).

With praise on our lips from a heart of pure adoration, I have no need of religious rituals or symbols. I know I can be real and let my heart speak His praise. As the psalmist says, 'I will praise God's name in song and glorify him with thanksgiving. This will please the LORD more than ... a bull with its horns and hoofs.' (Psalm 69:30-31).

The Father is always looking for those who will worship Him in Spirit and in truth. Truth includes the attitude of our heart even more than saying the 'right' words. Remember the Pharisee who went to the temple to pray and spoke about himself, his religious observance and how 'good' he was? Alongside him was a man who knew he was a sinner and cried out to God for mercy and forgiveness. The latter went home blessed and forgiven. We can all know the same peace and confidence. Paul tells the believers in Colossae that his prayers for them are that they may 'live a

The Pursuit of Pleasure

life worthy of the Lord and please him in every way' (Colossians 1:10). This is not only personal growth and satisfaction. It is also the commission we have been entrusted with.

God spoke to the Jews who were settled in their own lives and comfortable homes, while the temple lay in ruins. He commanded them to take note and think carefully about the situation they were in. He told them to go and collect the timbers needed to rebuild and complete the derelict temple. God said this was so He could take pleasure in it and be honoured. The story, in Haggai, also reveals the disappointment and dissatisfaction the people were feeling and experiencing because of this lack. Their neglect of God was having repercussions in their own lives. The psalmist, in Psalm 37, tells us that when we delight ourselves in the Lord He will give us the desires of our hearts. This is not a 'trade-off' deal. God knows the heart. He sees when we are trying to get something out of Him and confessing our love and devotion as a means of getting it. He cannot be fooled. He is looking for worshippers who will worship Him in truth, as well as in the Spirit. I think that can include those moments when we want to say, 'God, I feel really fed up.' He knows we are even before we tell Him. We gain nothing by pretending and everything by being honest and open. It is OK to tell God about the disappointments, the shock, the pain, the lack of understanding, and anything else that is real at the time. His arms are strong enough to carry us and His heart big enough to love us through it all. This is also worship. We are turning in faith, even though we may not feel very full of faith, to our Father with whatever is pressing on our hearts. That is acknowledging Him as sufficient in His grace and goodness for us to spill all our pain at His feet. The very turning to God is of itself an expression of faith, of trust in Him.

The teaching of the New Testament makes it abundantly

clear that we are God's house, God's temple. The abiding living quarters of the Holy Spirit. We read in Timothy, for instance, 'you will know how people ought to conduct themselves in God's household, which is the church of the living God, the pillar and foundation of the truth' (1 Timothy 3:15). Again, we see in Corinthians that 'we are the temple of the living God' (2 Corinthians 6:16). This is much more fully developed in my book Feasting on the Father (Exeter: Onwards and Upwards, 2012). God's pleasure is that we go up to the mountains and bring back the timber of our families, neighbours, friends, colleagues, and all who will listen, hear and respond to the good news of salvation in Jesus to the ends of the earth, so that His Church may be complete. It is more than this, though. It is about each one of us keeping a careful spiritual eye on the condition of our heart before God. We are loved beyond comprehension, from before we were born. We will be loved throughout eternity. Yet that does not absolve me from the obedience of devotion which refuses to excuse sinful attitudes and practices, or is careless to how I live. God has poured His love and Spirit into us as testimony that we have become righteous in Jesus. We are enabled to live in that righteousness through the same Holy Spirit. And if we sin, as John tells us, then we rush to our Advocate, our lawyer in the Holy Court of Justice, who defends us through His own blood sacrifice resulting in us being declared 'not guilty' and no record is kept of any wrong. This is our confidence and assurance in the covenant of grace in which we live.

I hear and read much about the imminent return of Jesus. I am as eager as the next man to see our glorious King come in triumph and majesty to claim His Bride and receive the honour due His name. For every knee to bow before Him and every tongue confess Him as Lord. Completing the building of His house achieves so much more than manoeuvring our minds through successive assumptions and speculations. I have books next to each other, quoting scriptures defending this view or that while seemingly contradicting each other. I read in the Bible that when the gospel has been preached throughout the whole world among every tribe, race, language and people group, then will come the end. I want to do my part in seeing this happen. What a joyful privilege and awesome responsibility. It is so important to be guided by the Holy Spirit in the unfolding of history and the signs that point to the culmination of things as we know them. It is so important to reach the lost with the good news of Jesus. I don't want the signs of the times, legitimate and outrageous, to deflect me from the high calling and honour of bringing an encounter with Jesus to those who are strangers to His love and grace. This gives God great pleasure.

Luke speaks of the great rejoicing in heaven over every repentant sinner. In the parable of the son who squanders his inheritance and ends up in shame and poverty there is such a great party and celebration when he returns home to his father. All of heaven joins in great praise and celebration, in rejoicing and excitement, when this happens. So passionate is our Father God for our hearts to be His! It was for this same joy that Jesus endured the cross, scorning its shame, that He might ascend, victorious, to the throne, there to await His darling Bride, the desire of His heart. Oh! What a day of heavenly delight when you bowed the knee and confessed Jesus as Lord and Saviour. Yes, you, you who feel so small, insignificant, such a failure and troublesome to God. Heaven has been celebrating you since that day. Partying over you being added to the Family as a chosen son or daughter of the King. He is your glory and the lifter of your head.

A very challenging and strange scene unfolds in the story of

God's Pleasure

Lazarus. Lazarus was a special friend of Jesus, as were his sisters, Martha and Mary. Lazarus is very ill. He is dying… and Jesus stays away. At this time of greatest need, Jesus chooses to remain apart from His friends. He knows Lazarus is going to die, and He allows it to happen. Now, Jesus testifies that He only did what He saw His Father doing and He only said what His Father gave to Him (John 5:19; 12:49).

So many of us are faced with tremendous challenges in life. Things happen which leave us feeling utterly bereft, deserted by God, filled with such pain that we do not know how we will get through the next hour. Jesus allowed this to happen to His friends. Indeed, He told His disciples that He was glad, for their sake, that He had not been there when Lazarus had died. The word used here for 'glad' is *'chairo'*. It means to rejoice, to be of good cheer. Jesus was rejoicing that He had not gone to Bethany to save his friend's life. Lazarus was dead, and Jesus is rejoicing. How strange this is to my understanding. The God of love is rejoicing at the death of a precious friend with all the inevitable grief, pain and questions. How do you get your head around that? There is a reason for this. Jesus knew it would bring faith to the disciples, the family, witnesses, and others. He also knew that this death was not the end of the story. He always sees the end from the beginning.

This is hard, challenging stuff. God walks with us through every trial, challenge, tragedy and trauma. Every seeming injustice and innocent pain felt, He knows. He shares it. I believe He invites us to partner with Him in these times in faith that He does actually know all about it.

I recall a dear friend recounting the experience of abuse she had suffered. She asked God, 'Where were You when that happened?' To which God replied, 'I was right there with you, alongside you, feeling your fear, pain, shame and horror.' This lady has recovered from that traumatic time and knows what Father God meant when He spoke those words to her damaged heart.

He has never promised that this life will be a bed of roses. We live in a sin-cursed world, with its ramifications. But we are never alone. And in God's heart there is rejoicing, there is delight that on the other side of these so challenging experiences, we will have been made more like Jesus through our faith in His goodness and good purposes towards us. The beauty of Jesus shines more brightly on our faces and from our hearts. He can see, before stuff hits us, the faith and hope that have grown through what we have been through. He knows that eternity in the fullness of His Presence and glory will wipe away every tear, heal every wound and remove all pain. Sorrow will be turned into joy, weakness into strength, anxiety into awe. There is rejoicing in heaven. This is the faith of love for God, knowing that in all things He is working for the good of those who love Him (see Romans 8:28). I know this because He tells us it is so in His precious love letter, the Bible.

Having a daughter who was born very severely mentally disabled, needing care 24/7, gives me a place from which to make this declaration. Having a wife whose life has been devastated by MS and fatigue, who, every day, lives with pain and limited activity, I am not in an ivory tower dispensing pious platitudes. I am in it, where it hurts. In choosing to trust we can know that 'my meditation [may] be pleasing to him, as I rejoice in the LORD' (Psalm 104:34). Therefore, as we choose to rest and trust in the goodness of our faithful God, we please Him. This also works for our benefit. John tells us that 'if our hearts do not condemn us, we have confidence before God and receive from him anything we ask, because we obey his commands and do what pleases him' (1 John 3:21–22). The words of the beautiful yet challenging worship song, penned by Matt Redman are so relevant here. In 'Blessed be Your Name' he speaks of us praising God when the sun shines down on us. That is easy. He speaks of praising God in the desert. This is more challenging. Then he leads us to praising God on the road of suffering, where pain is mixed into the praise. This is the most challenging thing to our faith. Yet those of us who are familiar with this song sing it faithfully and passionately every time. I confess to times when I sing it with tears as the reality strikes my heart afresh and the road of suffering is real. But God is my Father, He loves me with such passion. He has revealed Himself to me, I can do no other. I use the word 'challenge' many times here. I actually do not like the term. I much prefer to use the phrase: 'God gives us an invitation to partner with Him in the outworking of His pleasure in our lives.' A challenge always seems to me to be something extremely difficult, usually unattainable, frequently frightening, yet *Abba* God is constantly loving me, loving you. He is constantly for us, holding us, encouraging us, using everything we face as a means of making us more like Jesus.

In lives of submission and trust, we receive from Him everything we need. It is as we pursue Him, His kingdom and righteousness, above all else, that everything we need is added to us. Through it all we have this assurance that He is able to keep us from falling and to present us before His glorious Presence 'without fault and with great joy', therefore, 'to the Only God our Saviour be glory, majesty, power and authority, through Christ Jesus our Lord, before all ages, now and for evermore! Amen' (Jude 24–25). The end result is eternal, joyful glory in His Presence of Delight. The answer to my deepest desires. This is the pursuit of pleasure. Pleasure in our God.

The Pursuit of Pleasure

The Song of Songs expresses the passion and delight of God in us, the objects of His love. 'How beautiful you are and how pleasing, my love, with your delights!' (Song of Songs 7:6). This is what causes Father God to take great delight in you. To quiet you with His love and to rejoice over you by leaping and twirling in joyful abandon of love, He sings over you. I keep repeating these amazing words from the mouth of Zephaniah, so glorious are they to my heart.

- In what ways are you able to partner with Father God in reaching those who do not know Him? Why not pray for greater influence in their lives?
- Do you see yourself as someone so delightful to God? How do you think you can grow this consciousness?
- Does it excite you to seek out the purposes of God and partner with Him in seeing them fulfilled?

Chapter 3
Giving God's People Pleasure

'I delight greatly in the LORD; my soul rejoices in my God' (Isaiah 61:10).

'Delight greatly' means to enjoy.

'My soul rejoices in my God' equally means to leap and be joyful.

The greatest, deepest, most thrilling and exciting of experiences are found in encountering Jesus, and in encounters with Jesus.

Those words of Isaiah could be written, 'I greatly enjoy the Lord. My innermost being leaps about, joyfully, in my God.' What more can be said?

The psalmist claims that the fullness of joy is found and experienced in God's Presence (Psalm 16:11).

Both Isaiah and David lay claim to the wonder of experiencing the Living God for themselves. Just like Elijah, they were regular human beings, not special, or different, experiencing the same challenges and joys of everyday life that we face. So, there must be something worth searching for in their claims. This greatly valued pearl, worth selling everything to own, but never obtained by our own efforts. As blood-bought, born again children of God, through His grace lavished on us in Jesus, we live in His Presence. Jesus has promised us that He is always with us. Never for one moment are we separated from Him. In His lavish love and grace He has brought us into this place of abundant joy, even when we are not feeling it. I pray to grow more clearly into the experience of wonder and satisfaction.

Given that the fullness of joy is found in God's Presence, why is it that I so easily turn elsewhere to find what only He gives? I admit, even now, knowing how absolutely loved and secure in the Father I am, that I beat myself up about it, time and time again. I don't believe that is what God wants of me. I believe He simply wants the genuine repentance of my heart to be speedily confessed to Him. I am not suggesting an indifferent approach to what is not right yet in my life. But I am saying that 'trying harder' of itself will not achieve the desired end. It is only through repentance and embracing His grace in the truth of knowing that He is greater than everything assaulting me, that in faith I can prevail. If self-effort could achieve victory over sin, there would be no need for Jesus' sacrifice and poured-out blood. I recognise it follows, inevitably, that the fullness of joy and satisfaction cannot be experienced anywhere other than living in His Presence. It is in coming confessing to Him that demonstrates there is no eternal pleasure outside of *Abba* God. Father God invites us to drink from His delightful river. A river flowing with delights, exquisite wonders that excite, thrill and satisfy our deepest cravings, longings and needs. And this is not a river of one delight. It is a river of multiple expressions of His nature, heart and character, which flow to us from the abundant feast of His heart. Can we know anything more exquisitely fulfilling than to pause in His Presence and drink in His love, comfort, peace, joy, the power and rest of the realisation of His Presence? The sweet beauty of His name, the all-embracing fullness of His love?

This is how David expresses his heart towards God:

O God of my life,
I'm lovesick for you in this weary wilderness.

Giving God's People Pleasure

> I thirst with the deepest longings to love you more,
> With cravings in my heart that can't be described.
> Such yearning grips my soul for you, my God!
> I'm energized every time I enter
> Your heavenly sanctuary to seek more of your power
> And drink in more of your glory.
> For your tender mercies
> Mean more to me than life itself.
> How I love and praise you, God!
> Daily I will worship you
> Passionately and with all my heart.
> My arms will wave to you like banners of praise.
> I overflow with praise when I come before you,
> For the anointing of your presence
> Satisfies me like nothing else.
> You are such a rich banquet of pleasure to my soul.
> (Psalm 63:1–5, *The Passion Translation*)

Here we have David acknowledging all the pleasure and satisfaction he finds in God, while constantly aching for His Presence even more. He speaks of the delights of thinking of God when he lies awake at night (see verse 6). Of the joys of being in the sanctuary worshipping His God. Such is the experience this man knew of the faithfulness and Presence of God towards Him.

I wonder if the incident recorded in 1 Chronicles which tells of David's desire to drink the water from Jerusalem, while he is living in the cave of Adullam in the desert regions, is connected to this psalm. Several of his chief soldiers risk their lives to fetch some for him, and his response? He is so overwhelmed by their love and courage that he pours it out as an offering to God rather than taste it himself.

The Pursuit of Pleasure

What tremendous inspiration there is in David's words. Inspiration to know God in such a way. To be so taken up with Him as to crave His nearness and confess that nothing on earth can compare with Him. Have you ever experienced God so deeply that you physically ache for His Presence? You long, as a deer panting for water, to drink of His life-giving Spirit, the flowing rivers of grace? 'If you are thirsty,' said Jesus, 'come to me and drink!' (John 7:37, CEV). There is no need to drink anywhere else. I ask *Abba* God to create such a thirst, that David's testimony becomes as real for me. Someone has said that hunger is the currency of heaven. God is called 'my joy and my delight' by the psalmist (Psalm 43:4). Do you see God in this way? Is such an experience of God familiar or alien to your understanding and outlook? Does your heart leap with joy at this truth? Do these words fill you to bursting point with desire for more of God, or do you dismiss them as too 'out there' to be real for you?

I believe it depends so much on how much we long to know God, how well we experience Him moment by moment. As Peter proclaimed on the Day of Pentecost: 'You have made known to me the paths of life; you will fill me with joy in your presence' (Acts 2:28). The paths of life are the way directed by the Holy Spirit. This is the way, walk in it, is His instruction (see Isaiah 30:21). As He directs my steps He leads me beside quiet waters, and guides me in paths of righteousness. Even though we may find ourselves in valleys where the shadow of death is near, we have no need to fear. His comfort, security and strength are with us, each step we take. His steps keep us from the ways of harm and destruction. In this way we can be filled, in His Presence, with the joy of His Presence, and the joy of knowing His goodness towards us. We may look at the waves, or at the Maker and Master of the waves. He has truly given us everything in lavish abundance in Him, and as we live close to His heart, in faith, it becomes our increasing reality.

I cannot fail to see, from the Scriptures, that God Himself is displayed as the greatest of all delights to the human heart. The greatest joy to the soul of man. The most satisfying of experiences and fulfilling encounters we can ever know. My desire in this book is to excite such a longing for God that we will spend the rest of our lives in pursuit of this pearl beyond price. This treasure beyond comprehension.

'All I want is to sit in his shade, to taste and savour his delicious love … Oh! Give me something refreshing to eat – and quickly! Apricots, raisins – anything. I'm about to faint with love!' (Song of Songs 2:3,5, *The Message*).

It seems most reasonable to me that the precious gifts that are ours from the hand of God, must also hold this wonder and delight. The gifts from Delight surely have to be delightful gifts. For instance, Isaiah tells us that all who hold God's commands and walk in His covenant, will find joy in His house of prayer (see Isaiah 56:7). Their spiritual exercises will enjoy His acceptance and pleasure. In an internet conversation, recently, I read someone claiming that prayer is boring. God promises us joy in prayer. This is not surprising when we realise that our conversation is with Almighty God! The Creator of all that is seen and unseen. This 'Most to be desired above all the riches of the world' invites us into sweet communion with Him. To call Him '*Abba* Father'. To realise that God wants, He desires, to spend time and to communicate with you and me. We can hear and receive His words to our hearts and minds. Wow! What is this so amazing thing that God would speak with such as us? 'How sweet are your words to my taste, sweeter than honey to my mouth!' (Psalm 119:103). How can prayer be boring?

The Pursuit of Pleasure

Observing the disciplines of being a faithful lover and follower of Jesus, is such a sweet pleasure when the focus is on the object of such observances. Not on the 'have to' of doing them. Love only loves. When that love is received, it draws a willing response that expresses our love and gratitude. No 'have to' attached to this. A simple 'nothing can stop me' is the true heart response.

We read how the returning Israelites celebrated the Passover and Feast of Unleavened Bread for seven days, with great joy. God told Zechariah that fasting was to be a joyful occasion (see Zechariah 8:19). These are to be happy festivals for the people. Contrast this with the religious observations of the Pharisees in Jesus' time. They went about deliberately mournful. Making themselves look haggard so as to gain the respect and admiration of the people. They were roundly attacked by Jesus for this hypocritical, empty observance. God was not their sole focus. They were. Their shallow, showy form of religion was shown up for what it was. But for those who sought to bless and honour God, there was joy, happiness and satisfaction. I believe there is so much lost in our communion services for a lack of abundant joy. Yes, it is a serious thing to meditate on the death and resurrection of Jesus. To realise afresh the enormous price He paid so that we can know His love and forgiveness. To be called the children of God. But we celebrate this feast from the resurrection side of Calvary. Jesus is our risen Saviour; our glorious, victorious exalted One, the Lord of all lords and King of all kings; He is the hope of our hearts in His coming again to earth to claim His Bride. How can we not be full of joy as we take part in testifying to this every time we share bread and wine? May we always know the Father's delight in our true worship and the ways in which we express such devotion.

'At his tabernacle will I sacrifice with shouts of joy; I will sing

Giving God's People Pleasure

and make music to the Lord' (Psalm 27:6, NIV 1984).

The Scriptures assure us that when we look for God's truths to be directing our lives, that we desire to know His ways, that we embrace gratefully His every word and delight in them, so God derives pleasure. As Jeremiah testified, 'When your words came, I ate them; they were my joy and my heart's delight' (Jeremiah 15:16). I remember a few years ago, when my wife and I were considering moving abroad to the sunny Mediterranean, for the sake of her health. Suffering with MS is no fun and the warmth is something that greatly improves her well-being, and ability to function. We had a shortlist of potential new homes, Christian friends and a church waiting to welcome us, and the prospect of an exciting new chapter unfolding in our lives. Then one evening, during a meeting, both of us, without the other knowing, heard God say, 'Don't move to the sun.' We are so thankful that He spoke to us both. It made the decision to listen and obey much easier. As we chose to 'eat' this word, the joy and delight of following His heart, and not our own, is something that continues to this day. Life continues to be a daily challenge, but the beauty of His Presence and favour far outweighs the difficulties. Not everything He says is necessarily what we want to hear but, as with everything of His loving heart, we know it is better than our own choices. His loving disciplines bring us the righteousness and peace that cannot be enjoyed in any other way.

'Day after day they seek me out; they seem eager [or, and delight] to know my ways' (Isaiah 58:2). God's words of encouragement, inspiration, direction, correction, instruction, love and affirmation, should be a delight. Words we eagerly search the Scriptures to find; words we delight to 'eat', to take to heart and choose to live. His ways are the paths of life. He assures us that His thoughts and His ways are not the same as ours, but are so much more, they are glorious and righteous, so right and good for us. Outside of God's ways are ways of disaster, destruction and failure. They are cul-de-sacs leading nowhere. Yet His ways always provide for us to reach that end, then turn round and seek Him for the right way. He promises us that we 'will go out in joy and be led forth in peace' (Isaiah 55:12). Where we do not see this happening, is not an opportunity to give up, to doubt our Father's love. Rather it is an opportunity to press in deeper and stronger into His truth and declare it even when everything clamours against it. As the disciples said to Jesus, 'You have the words of eternal life' (John 6:68). Where else can we go?

God's words and ways, personified in the book of Proverbs as Wisdom, lead us to know what is right, is just and fair. A path to walk that is secure, peaceful and good. Such knowledge is meant to be a pleasure to our hearts and souls. By whoever, and however, walking the Christian walk was turned into a list of negatives and fruitless boredom, was most definitely not inspired by the Holy Spirit of God! Jesus came to give us abundant life (see John 10:10). A life of freedom, not imprisonment. What life are you building as a Christian? And how are you trying to achieve it? Jesus spoke of the wise builder who first of all found a secure foundation that would enable the house he was building to withstand whatever weather was thrown at it. In the same way, we read that 'Through wisdom is an house builded; and by understanding it is established: And by knowledge shall the chambers be filled with all precious and pleasant riches' (Proverbs 24:3–4, KJV). When our life is truly built on the Rock, which is Christ Jesus, and we allow the Master Builder to build His structure on that foundation, we can expect to find our lives littered with precious and pleasant riches of His grace. The memories of answered prayer; the times of heart-stopping worship when His Presence was so overwhelming that we could barely breathe; the delights of His voice telling us of His love and pleasure in us; the wonder of His hand providing our needs; His arms holding us in His peace, and a myriad of other memorial stones dotted across our life tracing the faithfulness of Almighty God, our *Abba* Father. This is the reward for those who embrace His truth and choose to walk in it.

The psalmist declares that those who walk in the light of God's Presence rejoice in His name all day long. The path of righteousness leads to rejoicing. As one preacher has said, God does not call us to holiness to keep us from pleasure. It is a call to experience fullness of pleasure in God's presence. That is something to sing and shout about! Rejoicing in the One who is known and loved for His goodness, whose very name causes joy. This is something more than simply enjoying the sound of God's name. It is that strength of faith which knows that His name opens and closes doors; releases life, healing, breakthrough, comfort and victory. The name that causes jumping about in exuberance. It is the Hebrew word *'Gul'* or *'Gil'*, mentioned earlier. How disrespectful it can be when God is referred to as 'Him upstairs' or the 'Big man in the sky', or some similar name. How much more so when it comes from the lips of those professing to be Christians.

'Give thanks to the LORD, call on his name … and proclaim that his name is exalted' (Isaiah 12:4, NIV 1984). Daniel in his great hymn of praise attributes the actions and qualities of God to be intricately joined to His name. And is it not so? 'Praise be to the name of God, for ever and ever; wisdom and power are his. He changes times and seasons; he deposes kings and raises up others. He gives wisdom to the wise and knowledge to the discerning. He reveals deep and hidden things; he knows what lies in darkness, and light dwells with him' (Daniel 2:20–22).

In the early days of the Church we read about the seven sons of Sceva, one of the chief priests, who attempted to use Jesus' name to cast out demons. They were overwhelmed, beaten and humiliated by the possessed man, and fled the encounter. Paul was demonstrating the power of Jesus' name, in miraculous ways. When this incident became known, the people were amazed and fearful because Jesus' name in the hearts and mouths of His disciples was effective for salvation and deliverance, but in the mouths of others, empty, so the power of His name was demonstrated. This led to many becoming Christians and turning from their superstitious magic. Possibly up to £8,000 of magic books and artefacts were publicly burned in Ephesus. Jesus' name is never a superstitious fetish to be conjured up for our own ends. He is God, Almighty, holy, in whose name we are to live and rejoice as His lovers and followers.

'You exalted me above my foes; from a violent man you rescued me. Therefore I will praise you, LORD, among the nations; I will sing the praises of your name' (Psalm 18:48–49). It is at the name of Jesus that every knee will bow, in heaven, on earth and under the earth, and every tongue will confess that Jesus Christ is Lord, to the glory of God the Father. Jesus has the name that is greater, higher, more powerful, worthy and exalted than any other. It is in His name that we can continually offer to the Father our sacrifices of praise. The fruit of lips that confess His name.

What makes this a sacrifice? The Greek word used, *'Thusia'*, speaks of a slaughtered animal. It speaks of the ritual slaughter at the altar to give an offering for sin. It is the same word as used in Romans 12:1 where we are exhorted to offer our bodies as living sacrifices to God. This must be praise that costs us something. The text speaks of a continual offering of praise. Not only when

Giving God's People Pleasure

everything is fine in our world, but also when there is pain and tears, darkness and doubt. This calls for a strong resolve that whatever hits us, we will praise God for who He is, for His unfailing love and faithfulness. This is the pleasure and comfort of those who truly know their God. I grew up with that precious hymn, 'How sweet the name of Jesus sounds in a believer's ear! It soothes our sorrows, heals our wounds, and drives away his fear' (John Newton, 1725–1807). Why this strong resolve? Because of knowing the grace gift of salvation. The gift of new life in Jesus, because of the unfathomable, outrageous love seen in the sinless, spotless Lamb of God, slain for us.

Isaiah's poem speaks of our joy in drinking deeply and satisfyingly of this wonderful love. 'The LORD, is my strength and my song; he has become my salvation. With joy you will draw water from the wells of salvation' (Isaiah 12:2–3, NIV 1984). Our joy is in receiving this great salvation. Even as we stand appalled at all that Jesus submitted Himself to, in the knowledge that it was all for our sake, we are able to embrace, with joy, the good life that is now ours. We are forgiven, cleansed, made new from the inside out. It speaks of how precious we are to God. How He chose us before He laid the foundations of the earth to be the objects of His love and delight, as His beloved children.

King David, in his despair over his sin, cried to God 'Restore to me the joy of your salvation' (Psalm 51:12). Joy is found in salvation. A salvation which brings us into God's family and kingdom. It makes us heirs alongside Jesus. It is a kingdom distinguished by joy, as well as righteousness and peace. Joy is to be the habitat of God's kingdom people. In another great song, Isaiah paints a picture of this joy. The joy that comes with life, with renewed zeal, and that pathway on which our feet are established as we come to the kingdom crowned with everlasting joy. Joy which overtakes and overwhelms us, such that sorrow and sighing will be experienced no more (see Isaiah 35:10).

This is the great good news. News to be trumpeted from the rooftops across every street, town and nation until all have heard, 'This is the God who loves you.'

Isaiah is the prophet who had a startling revelation of God and His glory. A revelation which caused him to weep over his wretchedness until an angel touched his lips. This freed him from the degradation of his sinful state and catapulted him to be the mouthpiece of God to the nation. No wonder he glories so much in God's great salvation. He has known it for himself. Seen and felt the power of God's grace and love creating him a new man for God. So, fearlessly he proclaims God's love for His people, more than once declaring God's salvation as the basis of God's ongoing faithfulness. 'This is our God; we trusted in him, and he saved us.

This is the LORD, we trusted in him; let us rejoice and be glad in his salvation' (Isaiah 25:9).

Isaiah is so caught up in this glorious truth that his words tumble over one another. The Hebrew he used here gives us meanings of 'be glad, rejoice, joy in, shine, joy, in His salvation'. What an overflow of wonder and delight in the reality of God's salvation love towards us.

The whole salvation story is filled with joy. That deep, secure, assurance pleasure to be found in the Father and His precious promises, and the wonders He displays on our behalf and through us in the lives of others. The birth of John the Baptist; the news of Mary's pregnancy when she met Elizabeth; the proclamation of the birth of Jesus, 'good news of great joy' (Luke 2:10, NIV 1984); the joy associated with the resurrected Jesus. The whole salvation event is undergirded and covered in a canopy of joy.

Giving God's People Pleasure

I confess I carry a banner in my heart. A banner that desires to see joy restored right across the Christian Church. Is it because we find ourselves so often struggling to keep our focus on Jesus, rather than on the circumstances we find ourselves in, that this missing dynamic of the good news seems lost so often?

Not only is our salvation a great source of joy, but the whole of the new life relationship with the Father is to be a life of joy, a life of pleasure. This is His desire for us to enjoy. Jesus spoke to His disciples and His teaching, His words of life, were such that they would know His joy, and their joy would be completed. Total joy through the truths that Jesus taught. I cannot emphasise enough the importance, as well as the pleasure of getting to know the Bible. Allowing its truths to reveal God's nature and heart towards me is something I look forward to every time I open my Bible. Growing in Him through taking His word to heart and choosing to believe it and seeking to walk in it. This brings the joy that Jesus spoke of. God promises us joy in place of mourning. He promises us, despite the challenges and persecutions we face, that our heavenly reward is great and a cause of great rejoicing. We have this pleasure to look forward to as we choose to believe and take to heart His precious teaching.

'Praise be to the God and Father of our Lord Jesus Christ! In his great mercy he has given us new birth into a living hope through the resurrection of Jesus Christ from the dead, and into an inheritance that can never perish, spoil or fade, kept in heaven for you, who through faith are shielded by God's power until the coming of the salvation that is ready to be revealed in the last time. In this you greatly rejoice, though now for a little while you may have had to suffer grief in all kinds of trials. These have come so that your faith – of greater worth than gold, which perishes even though refined by fire – may be proved genuine and

The Pursuit of Pleasure

may result in praise, glory and honour when Jesus is revealed. Though you have not seen him, you love him; and even though you do not see him now, you believe in him and are filled with an inexpressible and glorious joy, for you are receiving the goal of your faith, the salvation of your souls' (1 Peter 1:3–9, NIV 1984). These words were written to believers who lived in the shadow of such persecution. Some of them losing their lives in the fire as human torches to entertain Emperor Nero. I pray we may grow in devotion and overwhelming thanksgiving for the love and life we have received in Jesus to such a place where a laid-down life is embraced in the certainty of great pleasure in the Father and His perfect love.

'The ransomed of the LORD will return. They will enter Zion with singing; everlasting joy will crown their heads. Gladness and joy will overtake them, and sorrow and sighing will flee away' (Isaiah 35:10, NIV 1984). So great is the joyful pleasure of the salvation found in the Father that the authors of Scripture struggle to find words that can adequately express what it is really like. We can look forward to an eternity of total delight in the fullest freedom of holy life in Jesus.

Paul is so overwhelmed by this revelation that the events of his life as a servant missionary of God, sold out every moment of every day to the cause of making Jesus known, are termed as 'light and momentary troubles' (2 Corinthians 4:17). Troubles being used to achieve this glory. This is the Paul who was stoned to within an inch of his life. Beaten, whipped several times, shipwrecked three times, in danger from bandits when travelling around the Mediterranean nations. He was also imprisoned. Yet he called all this 'light and momentary troubles'. Why? And how? Simply because his heart was so passionate for God, the force of pleasure and delight in him was God. It was all worth it for the

Giving God's People Pleasure

sake of God's pleasure; for the sake of pleasing His Lord. And also the experiences of knowing God's pleasure in him as a faithful servant and the joy of living in such a close relationship. Add to this the pursuit of attaining his goal – everlasting life in Jesus.

How tightly do the things of this life hold your heart? How free is your heart to love God with such a burning passion that you will only ever be satisfied with His Presence?

A question arises in this context, namely: 'Isn't it selfish to pursue pleasure? Joy?'

I believe through the pages you have just read it is clear to see that all the delight and joy expressed and experienced is found in God. Surely if such pleasure is to be experienced in the Christian life as we fellowship with God, it has to be good and healthy pleasure. The Bible itself tells us to go after joy, to pursue delight. 'Delight yourself in the LORD', says the psalmist, promising that the desires of our hearts will be satisfied (Psalm 37, NIV 1984). God promises us that in His Presence is all the joy we could possibly every desire.

I remember reading an article by Andrew Wilson in *Christianity* magazine (July 2012) in which he said that what was supposed to be unspeakable joy had somehow turned into uncomfortable duty (my paraphrase). How sad that our God-given heritage has descended into a dull duty which did not fit well into the testimony of Scripture. We are always looking for pleasure in life, so why does it become selfish to look for it in God? We are told to always rejoice in the Lord. The Gospels abound with examples of people who really enjoyed being with Jesus. It is inevitable, since in Him all joy is found. He is the fountain of life. I believe people enjoyed being with Jesus because His acceptance, love and life-giving words brought a wholeness, a cleansing and sense of 'home'. I believe we too may enjoy such a time with Him. Joy

The Pursuit of Pleasure

exists because God exists. Joy is an expression of who God is and what His kingdom is like.

Therefore I urge you to reject any thoughts of it being selfish, and pursue all the pleasure you could possibly want in your pursuit of the heart of God and His will. It is not a bed of roses in most instances, but the overall testimony of people in the Bible who have pursued God, is that He is worth it.

- The good things that bring pleasure in your life fulfil a legitimate need. How do you think Jesus enhances that pleasure?
- Are you able to have fullness of pleasure without Jesus?
- Will you seek Him for the fulfilment of the pleasure He offers?

Chapter 4
Pressure and Pleasure

I want to turn our minds to a most challenging theme of Scripture. James puts it like this: 'Consider it pure joy, my brothers and sisters, whenever you face trials of many kinds' (James 1:2). How do we learn to have joy when we find ourselves under unwanted pressures?

We all know how easy it is to bless God and be full of thanks when everything is as it should be. We are secure, provided for, popular, successful, or even just getting by without too much hassle. We are coping. We would admit that a little more money would make things easier; the children could always behave better; our marriages could always do with a little more love and consideration, church is OK, but overall, we manage. But when we face the challenge of God's demand that we find joy in hardships, well, that's going too far! Don't you sometimes feel, 'It's OK for You God, You try standing in the unemployment line', or 'How would You feel if one of Your children was desperately sick, or has gone off the rails and is mixing with those who are pulling them down into drugs, loose living and indifference?' Joy in death? Or divorce? Are You kidding me?

How, and where, do we find this promised joy in such situations? How do we stand as believers against the animosity of colleagues, or family, because of our confession of Jesus as Lord and Saviour? In these times, don't you find that the words of James seem to mock you? To make you feel defeated and useless as a Christian, crushed by the inability to embrace and experience this elusive joy? Where is this place? Is it real? Can we really know such a joy when everything precious to us seems to be falling through our fingers?

The death of James is depicted by Josephus, the great historian of the time, as a stoning. He is also said to have been thrown off the pinnacle of the temple for refusing to speak against Jesus. However it happened, and it may have included both, it is apparent that James walked the walk he spoke about. I am horrified these days as I see on TV the evidence of Christians being martyred for their faith at the hands of religious extremists. Now, it would be wrong to put yourself down in the assumption that you could not endure the same thing. I believe we should simply trust God for how we would be if we found ourselves in a similar position. 'Sufficient unto the day' (KJV) are the words of Jesus. 'Do not worry about tomorrow, for tomorrow will worry about itself' (Matthew 6:34).

So, as I follow James in his encouragement, I find a clue as to why he says we should consider it such a joy when these trials are upon us. In James 1:3–4 he says 'because' – he is giving us the reason – 'because you know that the testing of your faith produces perseverance. Let perseverance finish its work so that you may be mature and complete, not lacking anything.' Do you know? Is your faith in God such that when the trials come, you have confidence in Him and His promises, whatever is happening? This is the essence of being a lover and follower of Jesus. A true believer. A believer is someone who believes!

Where does this knowing come from? There is such confidence in James' words. There is assurance and good reason to consider it 'pure joy' when your back is against the wall. It comes from the reality of knowing who Jesus really is. This is no ascetic world view or stoic philosophy. This is the knowing of Jesus as the risen and exalted King of Glory. The One who has triumphed over sin, death and hell. This is the Saviour who, at Calvary, fully and comprehensively fulfilled His eternal purpose as the Lamb of God who takes away the sin of the world. This is the Same One who promises that a trial 'has not taken you except what is common to mankind: but God is faithful, who will not permit you to be tested beyond what you are able, and therefore He will then in the test make you able to patiently bear the way out' (Rev William J. Morford, *The One New Man Bible*, Travelers Rest, SC: True Potential, 2012. Copyright 2011). Most translations speak of an escape, or God providing a way out. But that is not the literal meaning, a meaning which much more accurately conforms to what we actually experience. It is rare to escape, or see a wide open door with a sign saying 'RUN'.

These trials are in effect tests or opportunities from heaven which force us to choose either God's will, or our own natural response. Standing in faith enables a witness to the world that God's power is real in us. God knows already how we will respond. He has always known with every saint who has faced such trials. It is, as James says, transforming us (James 1:3–4). These trials, used by God to grow us, are set in the context of the Love that promises in every situation to be working them all together for our good as those who love Him, whom He has called to Himself. Also the Love that promises to be with us in the trial, because He has promised that He will never ever leave us or forsake us, not even for a moment. In our deepest struggles, the Holy Spirit is in us and upon us to empower us to endure. As the psalmist said, 'Even though I walk through the valley of the shadow of death, I will fear no evil, for you are with me' (Psalm 23:4, NIV 1984). He gives us assurance that we can feast on His

The Pursuit of Pleasure

precious provision of grace, whatever is against us.

As I write this I see the faces of two dear friends who at this time have endured five years of the most diabolical assaults of cancer. Many surgical procedures, unbelievable pain, brushes with death and the greatest challenges to their dynamic faith in God. Yet they stand. Having been knocked down, they get up. Knocked down again, they stand upright again, in faith. I cannot get away from their plight. I simply submit to Father God who, in His love, is walking with them on this pathway, leading them deeper into His heart.

So, come with me, as I attempt to look at this very challenging word.

Paul is known for the things he endured for the sake of Jesus. His experiences of hardship and extreme trial are well documented in the Bible. He outlines a small part of this in his writings to the believers in Corinth. He graphically speaks of being hard pressed; persecuted; struck down; always carrying the death of Jesus in his body, so that others may receive the life of Jesus. He concludes the passage with these words: 'we know that the one who raised the Lord Jesus from the dead will also raise us with Jesus and present us with you to himself. ... Therefore we do not lose heart. Though outwardly we are wasting away, yet inwardly we are being renewed day by day. For our light and momentary troubles are achieving for us an eternal glory that far outweighs them all. So we fix our eyes not on what is seen, but on what is unseen, since what is seen is temporary, but what is unseen is eternal' (2 Corinthians 4:7–18).

He is sustained and inspired by the hope of Jesus. 'Christ in you, the hope of glory', as he said in Colossians 1:27. He is set on heaven. This earthly arena is so temporary to him. The problems so transient in comparison to the glorious inheritance of 'forever with the Lord'. This is the same place that James is speaking from. He too knows the magnitude of eternity with God, free from everything that fails, hurts, destroys and is unsatisfying. He has faith that God is perfecting the likeness of Jesus through every situation that is encountered. For both of them it is all about what is ahead. The prize, the high calling of God in Christ Jesus. 'The Holy Spirit testifies in every city, saying that chains and tribulations await me. But none of these things move me; nor do I count my life dear to myself, so that I may finish the race with joy, and the ministry which I received from the Lord Jesus, to testify to the gospel of the grace of God' (NKJV). The words of Paul as he says goodbye to the believers in Ephesus, Acts 20:22–24. Even though he knows what is waiting for him, he joyfully anticipates it all, in the knowledge that he is promised an eternal inheritance, kept in heaven, reserved, with his name on it, when everything of this life is over.

That saying about being so heavenly minded to be of no earthly use sounds so crass when confronted with biblical truth. Being heavenly minded empowers us to face whatever lies ahead. It empowers the most glorious willing sacrifice, joyfully given, of self, for the glory of God. It seems to me that a greater consciousness of heaven would be a grace to embrace for the days in which we live. We need to be less earth-bound. Less taken up with 'now' and more looking to what awaits us in Jesus. Yes, grab everything of today, it is a gift from God. Seize every opportunity to represent Jesus to the world. But keep the focus on what lies ahead. Press towards the mark for the prize of the upward call of God in Christ Jesus. It most certainly enabled the earliest saints to shut the mouths of lions, quench the fury of the flames, escape the edge of the sword, to be tortured, refusing to be released, being chained and put in prison, flogged, sawn in two, being destitute, persecuted, mistreated, so that they might gain a better resurrection (see Hebrews 11:33–40). What a testimony! How powerfully the earliest lovers of Jesus knew the truth of satisfaction in Jesus. I am so good at singing it. They lived and died it.

Peter wrote a letter to Christians in the churches in Pontus, Galatia, Cappadocia, Asia, and Bithynia, an area now part of northern Turkey. It was written at a time of tremendous persecution of Christians. This emanated from Rome under the Emperor Nero. As I mentioned above, he had used Christians as human torches to light the gardens for his barbecues. He encouraged the slaughter of Christians in the amphitheatres by wild animals, for entertainment. This news will have spread quickly among the churches throughout the Roman Empire. We have probably all heard the story of how Peter was crucified upside down as he thought himself unworthy to die the same way Jesus had. Into this terrifying ordeal he wrote these words 'Dear friends, do not be surprised at the painful trial you are suffering, as though something strange were happening to you. But rejoice that you participate in the sufferings of Christ, so that you may be overjoyed when his glory is revealed. If you are insulted because of the name of Christ, you are blessed, for the Spirit of glory and of God rests on you. … if you suffer as a Christian, do not be ashamed, but praise God that you bear that name' (1 Peter 4:12–16, NIV 1984).

James, Paul and Peter, all familiar with suffering for the name of Jesus, each of them writing the same encouragement, rejoice! Be full of joy! I am reminded that James tells us that Elijah was just a regular person, like each of us, like Paul, like Peter. These men did not live some sort of special life in God. They felt the same as we do. They had their fears, doubts and failings. But the revelation of Jesus in their hearts and minds so captivated them that everything paled before His glory and love. He was most certainly worth it all.

There is no avoiding this Spirit-given attitude, 'Jesus truly is everything to me. His kingdom and glory are all I live for.' Do you know Jesus to be such a delight? The events of 9/11 demonstrated so dramatically that people will give their lives, willingly, for a cause, in the hope of something. The something that, in truth, is only found in Jesus. If people are so willing and hold their lives so loosely in the pursuit of futility, how much more should the blood-bought sons and daughters of God be ready to joyfully live and die for Him? How enraptured with Jesus are we?

I believe that in no more than a generation this world would be transformed if those confessing Jesus as Lord lived with this delight, this awestruck heart of amazing wonder and glorious passion. Being compelled by it to count their own lives as nothing in comparison.

Not only do we need a constant vision of heaven, but we also need a strong consciousness of the salvation given us through Jesus. I still remember the wonder that broke in on me, over fifty years ago, in the realisation of such a great salvation. 'Oh, who am I that for my sake, my Lord should take frail flesh and die?' (My Song is Love Unknown, Samuel Crossman, 1623–83).

Do you equally remember the revelation of how deep is the darkness of sin? Having been brought from death to life; 'from the dominion of darkness ... into the kingdom of the Son he loves' (Colossians 1:13), do you look back and realise how vile and destructive is the life lived outside of salvation? Even though such a life can have its pleasures, such pleasures are pleasures which lead to death should they inhibit the revelation of Jesus. They are pleasures which are fleeting and unsatisfying. Pleasures

The Pursuit of Pleasure

which leave an emptiness which fiercely looks for greater pleasure. It is like an addiction. An addiction that can never replace Jesus and His love. It is the pleasures which Moses refused to embrace so that he was free to embrace the reward of knowing God (Hebrews 11:25). The Bible makes it clear that there is pleasure in sin. Why else would we do it? We do it because we enjoy it, at the time. Also, as slaves to sin, we are, in reality, powerless not to sin. But from the position of salvation and life in God through Jesus, we are able to see the borders of bondage and all the destructive consequences which fill our news bulletins day after day.

Death to life, darkness to the kingdom of love and light. I don't know what your life looked like before Jesus became real to you. Mine was, outwardly, a good life. I was an obedient child. A caring person. Generally honest. Brought up in the church, familiar with the Bible and many of its passages. But when I stand in front of the holiness of God, I see a different 'me'. A 'me' who hides from himself the thoughts of his heart, who finds ways of excusing his attitudes and behaviour. 'I'm only human, after all,' and such things. Well, that is why God shows us His love so blatantly in Jesus. To transform us from being 'only human' to being Spirit-filled sons and daughters of God. The indescribable horrors of the crucifixion demonstrate the depravity of sin in us all, as well as the staggering immensity of God's love, and our worth to Him. Oh, the delight of rescue! The wonder of being so wonderfully wanted by *Abba* God that He came to our place to take us to His.

> Blessed assurance, Jesus is mine
> O what a foretaste of glory divine
> Heir of salvation, purchase of God
> Born of His Spirit, washed in His blood …

Pressure and Pleasure

This is my story, this is my song
Praising my Savior all the day long
(Fanny J. Crosby, 1820–1915)

The believers in Thessalonica knew this so well. 'For we know brothers and sisters loved of God, that he has chosen you, because our gospel came to you not simply with words but also with power, with the Holy Spirit and deep conviction. You know how we lived among you for your sake. You became imitators of us and of the Lord, for your welcomed the message in the midst of severe suffering with the joy given by the Holy Spirit. And so you became a model to all the believers in Macedonia and Achaia' (1 Thessalonians 1:4–7). The joyful receiving of the gospel far exceeded the sufferings they experienced as a consequence. This was a community of believers born in the cauldron of adversity and persecution, as outlined in Acts chapter 17. Such is the joy of new life in Jesus that they gained a substantial reputation which caused others to imitate their faith throughout the region. I wonder what impact a group of joyful, thankful, heaven-gazing people might have among their community and even across their town or city, today. As Christians, born-again lovers and followers of Jesus, we have this unique expectancy. Jesus is coming again! He promised He would be back, and His word cannot fail. Surely this is enough in itself to cause us to set our hearts (affections) on things above, where Christ is seated at the right hand of God. With our minds fixed on things above, not on the things of this passing world. Because when Christ does appear, we will also appear with Him, in glory.

Yes, the reality of heaven, of the return of Jesus, of our eternal destiny and security in Him, give cause to know that all the things of this life, traumatic as some are, are temporary, and in the gracious love of *Abba* God, more perfectly equip us for this glorious celebration.

Paul also saw the price of the salvation and maturing of believers as a greater joy than the trials involved in bringing that about. Such was his love for the lost, his love for the saved, that he gladly endured all that was necessary to fulfil his high calling in God. To the Corinthians he said, 'You have such a place in our hearts that we would live or die with you. I have great confidence in you; I take great pride in you. I am greatly encouraged; in all our troubles my joy knows no bounds' (2 Corinthians 7:3–4, NIV 1984). To the Philippians, a letter written from prison, where he was for the sake of the gospel, he declares: 'Do everything without complaining or arguing, so that you may become blameless and pure, children of God without fault in a crooked and depraved generation, in which you shine like stars in the universe as you hold out the word of life – in order that I may boast on the day of Christ that I did not run or labour for nothing. But even if I am being poured out like a drink offering on the sacrifice and service coming from your faith, I am glad and rejoice with all of you. So you too should be glad and rejoice with me' (Philippians 2:14–18). No word of complaint. No 'Poor old me, doing all this for God and look what He does to me. I don't deserve this, it's not fair'. These words speak for themselves. His life counts as nothing to him for the sake of the consolidating and maturing of his spiritual children. Can we find such an affection for one another that our time, our money and possessions, our energy and abilities are at the disposal of the saints with whom we share our lives? This is how Jesus is glorified that we show *agape* towards one another.

Can we find such affection for the 'not yet Christian' we meet in our daily life? Such that we love the one in front of us to show them what Jesus looks like in our generation? And to do it joyfully? Look again at the testimony of the Macedonian believers when they knew of the needs of their brothers and sisters. 'In the midst of a very severe trial', we read 'their overflowing joy and their extreme poverty welled up in rich generosity. For I testify that they gave as much as they were able, and even beyond their ability. Entirely on their own, they urgently pleaded with us for the privilege of sharing in this service to the Lord's people' (2 Corinthians 8:2-4). How this speaks of transformed hearts which were so caught up in the wonder and joy of Jesus and His salvation life that joyful abundant generosity became so natural to them! They loved their fellow believers to the point of great personal cost. This was birthed in love for God and wonder and gratitude at so great a salvation. Beyond the bounty of their needed gift is the giving of themselves, first to God, then to the Christian family wherever it is living. This is Paul's testimony of them in the next few verses. Pleasure experienced in the pressure of their own poverty and severe trials. How? And why? Because of adoration of the Father overflowing in love for fellow believers. Who among us knows this pleasure? Who is willing to pursuit it?

Loving our Christian family extends to those who have taken up responsibility under God to care for and lead our fellowships. I believe burnout is an insult to Jesus' promise that His yoke is easy and His burden light (see Matthew 11:30). In fact the sense of the language here suggests that His burden is as light as a feather, an undetectable weight we choose to bear. Yet so many Christian leaders live in permanent stress, worry, fatigue, oppression and loneliness. So many take on tasks that others could do. Many have such loving hearts that they struggle to ever say 'no' and pile more on their own plate, finding there are not enough hours in the day. Hebrews 13:17 tells us: 'Obey your leaders and submit to their authority. They keep watch over you as men who must give an account. Obey them so that their work will be a joy, not a burden, for that would be of no advantage to you' (NIV 1984). This highlights God's intention that shouldering God-given responsibilities of care, nurturing ministry and teaching, vision, encouragement and so on, are to be a joy. Sadly this frequently feels more like walking against a brick wall through thick treacle! Being crushed and broken, in despair, overwhelmed and often asking, 'What am I doing? There must be easier ways of making a living.' Believe me, I know, I've been in these situations. I've had other ministers sitting in my lounge, in tears, as they pour out the pain in which they find themselves.

But, a cautionary note. Our translators have failed to give us the best translation of this word 'obey'. This has led to much abuse and control as hurting leaders have hurt their flocks. 'Obey your leaders' does not mean 'I am your pastor/priest/vicar/elder, you do as I say'. It is a great sadness to me that there are many professing Christians who will not join themselves to local fellowships because of the hurt they have experienced at the hands of others. No one has a mandate to dictate conduct or belief to another. It does not mean that the person in the pulpit is six feet above contradiction. Nor does it mean they are easier to throw rocks at!

The Greek word translated 'obey' is *'peitho'*. It has several related meanings, none of which have to do with capitulation to commands. The word means 'to assure, to have confidence in, to have where one might trust, persuade, make one's friend, put one's trust in, be persuaded'. From this we can glean that the Greek word *'peitho'* does not mean obey, but rather, 'allow yourself to be persuaded through the confidence gained in relationship'. What a different approach that brings to us. Relationship is the basis of cooperation and honour, respect, encouragement and the building up of the Body of Christ. Relationship determines our responses. Not coercion or command. Based on love for my brothers and sisters I will give godly consideration to what is placed in front of me, and respond accordingly. This releases leaders, having discharged their responsibility, from the consequences in my life, although they are usually there to help me pick up the pieces. I base my consideration on knowing and walking together with the leadership. Seeing their integrity in God, their genuine love and care for me, the righteousness in which they live, I can conclude, 'Hey, what they are telling me is for my good.' They are not out to hurt me or pay me back for past failures, or anything negative like that. Because I know them, I know they would never deliberately lead me wrongly, never deliberately speak falsehood into my life. This is really what our word 'obey' conveys. This is all based on relationship. That is not surprising since it is God's *ecclesia*, His people being built together into a holy habitation of God in the Spirit. I pray that all in positions of responsibility would walk in this dimension of relationship ministry. *The Message* paraphrase words it this way: 'Be responsive to your pastoral leaders. Listen to their counsel. They are alert to the condition of your lives and work under the strict supervision of God. Contribute to the joy of their leadership, not its drudgery. Why would you want to make things harder for them?' (Hebrews 13:17). So, even when the words they speak into our lives appear to be harsh, we can have confidence in their love and recognise that 'No discipline seems pleasant at the time, but painful. Later on, however it produces a harvest of righteousness and peace for those who have been trained by it'. (Hebrews 12:11).

God is not a Santa Claus sprinkling Disney dust over all our difficulties to make them disappear. Those who speak love into our lives will not shrink back from doing so. 'Wounds from a friend can be trusted', as we read in Proverbs 27:6. Oh! For loving friends who will love me enough to speak truth to me so that I may walk more perfectly in the ways of God.

So, given that leaders are to minister in love through relationship, God has no other way, it means that those without leadership responsibilities are to encourage, support, lay down their lives, joyfully, and agree with them, in the awesome work God has called us, jointly, to co-labour in. We have no right to expect a level of behaviour and spiritual maturity from our leaders, which we are not prepared to pursue in our own lives. If we expect them to not lie, then we don't lie. If we expect them to sacrifice their time for us, then we must sacrifice our time for them and one another. If we expect them to be above reproach, we must also be above reproach. There is only one level of Christian righteousness. 'Be holy because I ... am holy (Leviticus 19:2). There is only one Body. We are all part of it. A body functions in complete unity within itself. 'Roast preacher' for Sunday dinner is never an option. Neither is backbiting, jealousy and gossip. Why would any child of God want to hurt or attack a fellow believer? Why would any of us want to throw rocks at the person in the pulpit? Does my body wilfully choose to hurt itself? Maybe if I am in such pain that I look for ways out. Ways of destruction to try to dull the ache and fear. But we are called to be united in cooperation with the Holy Spirit to see the pleasure of God fulfilled in His Church. It is for our good. It is for our pleasure since our delight is found in Him and doing what pleases Him. We have been made new in the Holy Spirit. We have no need for self-destruction. I dare to imagine and dream of the Church without fault, blemish, wrinkle or spot (see

Ephesians 5:27). Where God's canopy of love hangs over us as a covering of grace. Where we welcome His love to permeate every aspect of our relationships and life. So that the 'not yet Christian' community in which we live sees the light of the glory of God in the place of Christian unity. They will know we are Christians by the way we love one another.

The psalmist speaks of rejoicing and gladness when God brings restoration to His people. Once again the words used speak of this exuberant celebration. We are to find delight and joy in following the ways of God in every aspect of life. Nothing is outside of His promise, nothing outside His grace. Those who sow in tears will reap with songs of joy. It is Father's promise. I understand there are at least 7,000 promises of God in the Bible. Every one of them has its 'yes' in Jesus. Every one relevant to us as His beloved children. And God has power to do what He has promised (see Romans 4:21). Even though it may appear to be more like the valley of the shadow of death, He is still with us. He continues to comfort and strengthen us. At such times we can know the pleasure of who our Father is. We can experience the delight of His Presence and truth at work in us to bring us through still believing and loving Him.

This is no triumphalist platitude. This is truth based in the very essence of who God is. It is about choosing to live by faith in Him and His word. 'Weeping may remain for a night, but rejoicing comes in the morning' (Psalm 30:5, NIV 1984). *Abba* God has assured us that He will not allow us to be tested in any way beyond what He knows we can individually endure, and therefore in that trial He will make us to patiently be able to bear the way out (1 Corinthians 10:13). This is not about God giving us a quick get-out, an escape from the challenge. We all know that does not really happen. But He is promising that in His love

The Pursuit of Pleasure

and grace, He is going to empower us to walk through whatever it is and come out the other end intact spiritually. Then to realise we have matured in our faith and walk as a consequence of what we have been through. Jesus is always the answer. Turning to Him, even in the greatest trials, and particularly in the greatest trials, is our way of success. And that brings pleasure.

'Never let the size of your giant determine the size of your God', as someone has said.

I am not suggesting you jump about in joy that you have lost your job, or your child has been lost. That is not what this teaching is about. The promises of God are to be as a hedge around us. A hedge of love and grace. The eternal assurance in His ability, during our most challenging times. And, above all, to know that He is God, in whose heart we live. In whose hands we are held. And who is bringing us to our eternal home.

Abba God assures us that His joy is our strength. His joy in us. Jesus, while teaching about remaining and continuing in the reality of His love, tells us His teaching will bring His own joy into us thereby making our joy complete (John 15:11). God's kingdom is a kingdom of joy. Such that: 'Though the fig-tree does not bud and there are no grapes on the vines, though the olive crop fails and the fields produce no food, though there are no sheep in the sheepfold and no cattle in the stalls, *yet* I will rejoice in the LORD, I will be joyful in God my Saviour. The Sovereign LORD is my strength; he makes my feet like the feet of a deer, he enables me to tread on the heights' (Habakkuk 3:17–19, emphasis mine).

Is it worthwhile inserting the challenges in your life into this great affirmation of faith? I think it may be. Though my child has cancer; though my finances are in a mess; though I find myself trapped in an addiction; though my marriage is failing; though my church has split, or whatever they may be, yet, I will, I choose,

Pressure and Pleasure

by faith, to rejoice in the Lord. Such rejoicing is in who God is. It is not rejoicing because of the circumstances. That is folly. We are called by our loving Father to trust Him. To choose to focus on Him and His promises, not the circumstances.

Focusing our hearts, minds and affection on our God is what brings the joy which strengthens us in the trial. He knows the size of your mountain. He wants you to tell your mountain just how big your God is. The writer of Hebrews reminds the believers, 'Remember those earlier days after you received the light, when you stood your ground in a great contest in the face of suffering. Sometimes you were publicly exposed to insult and persecution; at other times you stood side by side with those who were so treated. You sympathised with those in prison and joyfully accepted the confiscation of your property, because you knew that you yourselves had better and lasting possessions' (Hebrews 10:32–34, NIV 1984). The strength and inspiration to endure, with joy, came from their hope of the future promises of God. This is the assurance of faith. It is seeing the invisible. It is having the evidence of what is not yet, deeply secured in the heart, based on the belief that God has said it, therefore it is so.

Many Christians across the world today are standing in this place because of fanatical religious extremism. They are yielding their lives to the sword in the certain knowledge that a far greater life is waiting in God. I believe our Father desires that we find this pleasure in times of great challenge.

At times it seems that there is no let-up to this sort of challenging life. We lurch from challenge to pressure moment, followed by crisis time. On top of this there are times when we experience the gracious discipline of our loving Father as well. I say 'gracious' since this discipline is for our good. We have known the disciplines of our earthly parents and, though painful at the time, we came to understand the love and purpose in them. Without discipline, the Bible tells us, we are as if illegitimate, fatherless ones. God's disciplines should cause us to know 'My Father loves me! This discipline I'm going through proves it!'. In all their individually tailored forms, they work holiness in us. This brings a harvest of righteousness and peace. Oh, how blessed is such an eternal perspective and focus!

Paul demonstrates what this looks like as he tells the believers in Corinth about the amazing heavenly visions he had. He tells them how God allowed something into his life to keep him from boasting about what a mega-Christian he was, travelling to the nations, saving people from an eternity without God; healing their bodies. Teaching the believers the way of the cross. I'm speaking of Paul joyfully embracing the discipline that came on his life through this 'thorn in his flesh' (see 2 Corinthians 12). Something to keep him from becoming boastful. If anyone had cause to boast, surely it was Paul. He gladly took hold of this and held it close to his heart, so that the weakness that kept him crying out to God for grace would enable God's power to more fully take possession of him. He sees the city whose Builder and Ruler is God. His weakness is irrelevant in comparison.

The realisation that God's power comes to fulfilment in human weakness causes him to know that the Holy Spirit is 'up to the job'. He boasts now in Jesus, not his own ability. 'Praise God, I can't do this! This means it can only be done through God's strength and power in me. To God's name be the glory.' He knows that his inability is God's opportunity. His delight, his pleasure, is experienced in the painful humbling realisation that 'all the bad stuff throws me back onto God who is my strength'. This means that only God can get the applause, the praise and the glory. Yes! May we also find that place in which we really know the peace of

Pressure and Pleasure

God that keeps our hearts and minds in Christ Jesus.

The 'secret', which is no secret, for Scripture abounds with this truth, is that living in the reality of God's loving Presence is the place to experience His joy the most. In this place we are able to prove in experiential power that there are abundant pleasures at His right hand. It is found in not being content with anything less than the place of deepest intimacy. It is in knowing Father God above all other desires and pursuits as the most to be desired and sought after.

'Apart from you I have no good thing' is the confession of King David, the psalmist (Psalm 16:2). King over all Israel. Rich beyond measure. Surrounded with the best of everything, yet confessing it all as nothing in comparison to knowing and living in God. Paul boasts the same thing. He counted everything as 'garbage' (Philippians 3:8) in comparison to knowing Christ Jesus. The nice home I've worked for, for years, garbage! The new car, garbage! My position in the community, garbage! The church, garbage! My bank account, garbage! Everything is seen as garbage when compared to knowing God. Even my health and peace of mind; even my family and friends; my children and grandchildren; my ministry, locally and nationally, even internationally, nothing can compare to knowing Jesus Christ. Jesus, the greatest, ultimate delight of the human heart.

Does this thought cause you to pause? To pause and ask, how can I know Jesus like this? Why is my experience of Him so small in comparison to David? To Paul? David and Paul were ordinary, regular people. Nothing special to set them apart for God's favour. Just like you and me. But, once God got hold of them, once their hearts were changed and their minds blown apart by the awesomeness of God and His incomprehensible love, they were lost, ruined to anything else. Ruined to any other life than chasing after God with all they had. Yes, they messed up. But that did not disqualify them. God does not disqualify us, we disqualify ourselves by a lack of hunger. It is those who hunger and those who thirst who are filled. Jesus said, 'If you are thirsty, come to me and drink!' (John 7:37, CEV). If someone is not thirsty, they will not drink. If someone is not hungry, they will not eat. If the things of this life satisfy, then carry on filling yourself with them.

To true lovers and followers of Jesus, I would ask, 'How can the things of this life compare to Jesus? Having tasted and found that He is good, where else would you want to feast?' And these words come back to pierce my heart every time I nibble at something else.

We have God's confirming word that every good and perfect gift is from Him (see James 1:17). Every blessing from His hand is to be appreciated and enjoyed. And we need to give Him thanks for all such gifts. This is not the issue. What I am striving to demonstrate is that nothing compares to Jesus. That being so, why look somewhere else for that which satisfies? 'LORD, you alone are my portion and my cup; you make my lot secure. The boundary lines have fallen for me in pleasant places; surely, I have a delightful inheritance' (Psalm 16:5–6). It is right and proper to acknowledge the grace of God in our lives. We are His beloved and He is ordering our steps. As I said earlier, all His promises are 'yes' in Jesus. Through His death and resurrection, Jesus became the hiding place for every broken, fearful, lost being on earth. He pours out the blessings of God upon us. He is the answer to the deepest needs and desires of everyone. Jesus is preparing for us an eternal dwelling place that far outweighs the most sumptuous mansion on earth. This is the faith of those who were overwhelmed by its truth that they abandoned everything to pursue God. Those who have endured in the certain hope that burned in their hearts. It was and is worth it all.

This is a recurring theme throughout the Scriptures. Sorrow turned to joy; death into life. The history of Israel in the Bible is a picture of this. From slavery in Egypt to the abundance of a land of their own. The prophets faithfully calling the nation back to God in the promise of His forgiveness and restoration. The exiles finding their way home. The rebuilding of the ruins of Jerusalem and the temple. Read afresh the book of Esther; see the utter calamity surrounding the exiled Jews – hours away from annihilation, until God steps in and they become the people of respect. A people whom others wish to join. They gained a royal seal of approval. Their deep sorrow was turned to extravagant joy.

We see it in Jesus. His bloodied body carrying all our sin, sorrow, pain, failure, shame, guilt and brokenness. Carrying it to the grave to leave it there destroyed, forever. Rising to life, the first of a completely new race. The adopted, chosen, redeemed community who have embraced this most staggering expression of love, and been transformed into the carriers of His glory. This divine exchange is beyond my comprehension, but within our experience. How great is the value you place on your salvation? That is the question. Is God so great as to be trusted come what may? So great as to be worthy of worship and devotion every moment of every day? The bottom line is that God is good. Always very good. Circumstances do not change Him. A true benchmark of our love for and growth in God is seen in our responses to the circumstances. He invites us to worship Him, to delight in Him. To find pleasure in Him whatever storms are raging around us. In our pursuit of Him we experience the pleasure of His Being even in the middle of the storm. That pleasure speaks peace into our hearts and minds.

The Pursuit of Pleasure

'But let all who take refuge in you be glad; let them ever sing for joy. Spread your protection over them, that those who love your name may rejoice in you. Surely, LORD, you bless the righteous; you surround them with your favour as with a shield' (Psalm 5:11–12).

Let me finish this chapter with some words from the mouth of Dr Helen Roseveare, an inspirational missionary in Congo for twenty years. She established medical centres and trained medical staff. She also experienced great suffering, including being imprisoned, beaten and raped. She said this was all 'small and transient in the greatness and permanence of the privilege'.

- Do you have any strategies for finding God in the difficulties and darkness?
- Do you know what it is like to praise God during the challenging times?
- How would you make it a lifestyle for yourself?

Chapter 5
Pleasure in One Another

> To dwell above with saints we love,
> Ah Yes! That will be glory.
> To dwell below with saints we know,
> Huh! That's a different story.
> (Author unknown)

We smile with that all too familiar, knowing smile. But must it be so? Should it be so? Is it possible for us to love one another the same way Jesus has loved us?

I believe it is. To begin with, Jesus commanded it. I cannot conceive of Jesus asking anything of us that we are not able to achieve. Add to that the many scriptural endorsements and encouragements to live the life of joyful, loving, delight-filled relationships. Paul spills his love for the believers in Philippi all over the pages of his letter to them with a joyful, unashamed abandon. He has such affection for them. He starts his letter by telling them how every time he thinks of them he is full of thanks and joy. They have captured his heart. It was in Philippi that he was whipped and imprisoned. Out of his suffering the church was born. He muses on his situation. 'I want out of here. I would much rather be with the Lord in His glory.' Who can blame him? Who wouldn't want the same thing? Yet, his love for them and his desire for their progress in the faith cause him to choose to stay among them. As he reflects on their attitudes and behaviour, the joy he already has in God is filled up even more. This is what causes the overflow of affection towards them, I believe. 'Make my joy complete by being like-minded, having the same love, being one in spirit and purpose' (2:2, NIV 1984).

Are we so connected in our local community of believers that we find such joy in the progress, obedience and humility of one another? Is it important to you that the believers around you grow in the Spirit? Does it flood your heart with pleasure as you hear them pray? See them in worship and witness their service?

'Love one another,' said Jesus in John 13. 'Love one another the same way I love you.' That way is the selfless way of laying down one's life, desires and ambitions for the benefit and good of other Christians.

How do you view the time when you will be gathered with the community of believers to which you belong, week by week? Do you delight in the possibility of: 'They devoted themselves to the apostles' teaching and to the fellowship, to the breaking of bread and to prayer ... All the believers were together and had everything in common. They sold property and possessions to give to anyone who had need. Every day they continued to meet together in the temple courts. They broke bread in their homes and ate together with glad and sincere hearts, praising God and enjoying the favour of all the people. And the Lord added to their number daily those who were being saved' (Acts 2:42–47). Or, does this picture make you want to turn and run in the opposite direction?

Meeting together, every day, to worship together; sharing their homes and food; breaking bread in the front room together; keeping their relationships strong, fresh and healthy; delighting in their new-found family. This is the result of the fullness of the Holy Spirit upon the lives of lovers and followers of Jesus. Is an hour or two on a Sunday morning enough? Is it as much as can be coped with? Is it all you feel you need?

If an hour or two on a Sunday morning equates with 'enough', I dare to suggest there is a very serious relationship gap and understanding of God gap, as well as a 'take it or leave it' gap in relation to what salvation truly means. I suggest the same applies to the other questions. Is it really possible that someone who has come to know Jesus as Lord and Saviour, who has the Holy Spirit of God within them, can be content with a couple of hours spent building their relationship with God? How do we really get to know Him if we can be as careless as to sideline His importance?

I believe it has never been about what I need, or want. I am convinced from Scripture that it is all about God. Being a Christian, a born-again lover and follower of Jesus, surely our foremost desire and compelling passion will be God, and what pleases Him? Is God happy and satisfied with a couple of hours on a Sunday morning? I know He delights in every moment we choose to meaningfully engage with Him.

I have a friend who lives in a state of desperate desire to know more of God. To spend more time with Him. I commented that God deeply desires the time they spend together. He jealously guards that time so that nothing and no one will be allowed to disturb this intimacy of love and longing. It is as if He looks at His watch and says, 'Three minutes, My beloved will be here in three minutes, I can't wait.' Do you sometimes find an uncomfortable sense of 'there must be more than this' even while going through the familiar forms of worship? Are the darts of Divine desire delving into the deepest depths of your soul, stirring a heart cry for the heart of the Father? Letting loose a longing for the loved ones to actually be the loving ones?

The greater the intimacy, the more intense the passion. The

more intense the passion, the greater the pursuit of the prize. Love and longing for God is reflected in love and longing for one another. Our love and longing for one another is reflected in the time we set aside to share Jesus with them. 'Love one another, as I have loved you.'

Paul goes so far as to call these Philippian saints his 'beloved', those 'much to be desired', as the Greek emphasis draws out. His longed-for, his joy that crowns his head with the glories of princely pride. They are his children in the Lord and his father heart is bursting with love, joy and pride, the sort that every true father knows. How much more will our heavenly Father, Abba God, the One who is with us, who is mighty to save and who takes great delight in us, the One who quiets us with His love and sings songs of extravagant joy over us with such abounding expressions of delight, find great joy and delight in us, His children? If we are so gorgeous and delightful in God's eyes, what prevents us from seeing it in ourselves and one another?

This deep affection and delight is not exclusive to the Christians in Philippi. Paul shares the same sentiments with the believers in Thessalonica. He tells them that they also are his joy, hope and crown in which he glories before God. They are the trophies of grace for whom all the struggles, pain and tears are worthwhile. I love the way the NIV expresses this as it states 'out of our intense longing we made every effort to see you' (1 Thessalonians 2:17). This intense longing also translates as 'over desire'. He has an overwhelming desire to be with his fellow believers. I long and pray for the Church today to be filled with those whose love, desire and delight for God and one another is as overwhelming.

'How can we thank God enough for you in return for all the joy we have in the presence of our God because of you?' (1 Thessalonians 3:9).

Pleasure in One Another

Do you have Christian friends to whom you can say: 'I long to see you, so that I may be filled with joy'? (2 Timothy 1:4). How can we cultivate such a deep delight and affection toward one another? I know we can choose to bless. I know we can pray with no regard to what has passed between us. I know we can choose to forgive and to see others as those for whom Jesus died. That alone reminds us that they are so precious in His sight. King David makes this observation: 'May those who delight in my vindication shout for joy and gladness; may they always say, "The LORD be exalted, who delights in the well-being of his servant"' (Psalm 35:27). He is acknowledging those who delight in his prosperity and well-being. I am reminded of the scripture which encourages us to weep with those who weep and rejoice with those who rejoice. I have always believed it is so much more a challenge to rejoice with those who rejoice. How does it feel when your 'desperately in need of a serious, expensive makeover' car is parked next to the friend who has a brand-new all-singing, all-dancing, gleaming model which simply oozes status and performance? Try rejoicing with him in that! Or you have just lost your job and a member of your church has just been promoted with a significant pay rise. Try rejoicing with him in that. Do we wish, work and pray for the prosperity of others? Or are we consumed with our own real and perceived needs?

There truly is great satisfaction in blessing others and watching them prosper. That tells me we have pleasure in blessing others while lifting our eyes off our own needs. Not blessing them does not change my situation. Blessing them may release something from heaven towards me.

What is it the psalmist longs for? The one thing He asks of God? It is to live all his life in the house of the Lord (see Psalm 27). His overwhelming desire is to be as close to God as possible.

For David that meant the Tent of Meeting. The one place that represented God's Presence among His people. Do you know a desire for God as intense as this? I ask because this points us even deeper into relationship. It does not need too much study to arrive at the truth that God's house is not bricks and mortar. Rather, it is people. Although I have developed this theme at length elsewhere, it still bears emphasising. I believe it is one of the most significant yet hidden truths of Scripture. So significant that when the Church at large gets hold of this dynamic truth, it will change the mind of believers in such a way as to seem like a tsunami of Holy Spirit, an avalanche of transformation of lifestyle and witness that will rock the Church and confound the community. We are the house of God. Every truly born again, Spirit-filled believer is a sanctuary in which God chooses to live by His Spirit. Every community of Christians is a sanctuary, a building made of living stones, to become such a spiritual house that the glory of God which filled and burst out of the temple that Solomon built, will be as something slight in comparison. Now, I know most believers hold to the theory of this truth, but how many of us embrace the reality and seek to live in the abounding blessing of it? The building exists to keep the weather off the Church and to help in its demonstration of God's love to the community around. Now, as we bring these two thoughts together, we find a God-given desire that His children will know Him, see Him and celebrate Him in one another. His Presence is among us as we come together. We show our love for Him by loving one another as if it were Jesus Himself in person among us. He desires that we love each other as He loves us. He desires that we long for each other's well-being and progress as He does our own.

What I am saying is that Jesus laid down His life unto death.

Pleasure in One Another

He rose again to become the Head of a brand-new race of people, the blood-bought community of lovers and followers of God. He poured out His glory on us so that we would catch His heart for those we are bound to in fellowship, carrying His passion which aches to spend all of life in company with fellow believers. As I do, I come seeking, finding and embracing Jesus as I love, serve and celebrate Him together with other believers. In the face of this, is it possible that an hour on a Sunday morning is sufficient? That we have 'done our duty' to God? Is it what Abba God is really looking for?

I am convinced that as the ecclesia grasps and grows in this truth, then all the shameful denominational divides will crumble to dust as believers, overflowing with Holy Spirit love and obedience, will find one another and see Jesus in place of a divisive label. The reality is that in your village, town or city, God has and sees only one Church. He has one Body of people in that place. One community of Christians. 'How good and pleasant [or pleasing to God] it is when God's people live together in unity!' says the psalmist in Psalm 133. Unity means being joined together, attached, inseparable. It is us being 'as one'. One Body, one Bride, one family, one building. Unity is the heart of God. The writer of the psalm continues with affirmations of great Holy Spirit anointing which saturates the whole. A relationship condition in which God is pleased to command His blessing of life for evermore.

Is there anyone who does not desire such grace outpouring? Grace lavished upon the community as it overflows from the believers and spreads out touching every facet of local life? In the Revelation of Jesus Christ, John writes letters to churches. Letters addressed to the church in Ephesus; the church in Smyrna; in Pergamum; the church in Thyatira, also in Sardis, in Philadelphia and in Laodicea. Notice he does not write to the church in Mark's house in Ephesus and the church in Andrew's house in Ephesus. No letter to the church in Alexander's house in Sardis. Each letter is sent to the whole Christian community in that town. The Church in that town, not the churches. I believe it is extremely urgent that we grasp this concept clearly and embrace it eagerly and without fear. How great the need for someone in your community to see and hear Abba God's heart and have the passion and courage to run with it. To own it for Jesus' sake. Christ is not divided. He is head over all things for the Church which is His body (see Ephesians 1:22–23). Not the churches which are His body. Nor is He actively head over everything calling itself and looking like His body which is not. It is the Church which is His body over which He rules in glory and passionate love and joy. Jesus is not broken or fragmented. We eat of one loaf, demonstrating the one sacrificial Lamb; one Saviour; one Body; one Bride; One kingdom with one king, one God and Father. Unity is the very heart of God. Unity is the prayer of Jesus. 'My prayer is ... that they may all be one, Father, just as you are in me and I am in you. May they also be in us so that the world may believe that you sent me. I have given them the glory that you gave me, that they may be one as we are one – I in them and you in me – so that they may they be brought to complete unity. Then the world will know that you sent me and have loved them even as you have loved me' (John 17:20–23).

I believe in the reality of this because Jesus has prayed it into being. The text tells us that the world will see and know the truth through such Oneness of believers held together in the same love Jesus enjoys. This says it is for today, not for some time in a future state of glory.

Here, now, on the earth, that the unbelievers will believe.

Pleasure in One Another

Is the spotless, wrinkle-free, stain-free Bride carrying the blemishes of broken fellowship in her bodice? Is her bouquet of flowers made up of lifeless, failed fellowships of stubborn hearts? Or is it the vibrant colours of countless caring, sharing, attached, inseparable communities? I believe it is our goal today, achievable through the laid-down lives of laid-down lovers, reaching out to each other in the Holy Spirit. One in the Spirit, even if not yet one in the faith. The abundant outpouring of Holy Spirit into captivated hearts, touching others whose submitted wills and one kingdom desire stimulate increase of love that demonstrates God to one another and the unsaved. With God all things are possible. When we know this is God's will for us all, we can pray knowing we are speaking His heart's desire into reality. My prayer is that we awaken to this desire of the Father. That we choose to pursue His heart. Pursuing His heart as we pursue love for, and delight in, one another. Why not me? Why not you?

At the sound of Mary's voice, Elizabeth testified that the baby in her womb leapt for joy. John went on to say that Jesus must increase and he became less and less significant and important in his day. His desire was to point people to Jesus and away from himself. Is Jesus everything to you? Is He really your deepest, greatest delight? I read of Jesus that His delight was to fulfil the will of the Father. It took Him to a cruel, inhumane, humiliating death on a tree at the hands of the ruling, occupying Romans. So intense was His desire to please His Father. We are called to follow Him, to have the same mind as He. To be willing to embrace the loss of all dignity in the eyes of men. To surrender all standing and achievement such that as Jesus' naked surrender to the will of the Father, we too may know that joy unspeakable in the Father's pleasure. Jesus became the first of a new race of citizens of heaven. What reward awaits our following in His footsteps?

The Pursuit of Pleasure

As Paul says, 'you who are strong ought to bear with the failings of the weak and not to please yourselves. Each of us should please his neighbour for his good, to build him up. For even Christ did not please Himself, but as it is written 'The insults of those who insult you have fallen on me' (Romans 15:1-3). Are there times when you fall into the trap of trying to please people, to dance to their tunes, rather than to please the Father? A soldier knows what it is to work to please his commanding officer. How much more we, who have a King to serve and give joy to? When I honestly look in the mirror, I know I find no deep, lasting pleasure in pleasing myself. But in serving others I am able to grow in the knowledge of God. Is the denomination you belong to, or the structures and rituals of your form of worship, or your programmes, your position within the church, or its standing in the Christian community, your preferences and reputation, of greater value to you than fulfilling the will of God to love one another as He has loved you? Are you prepared to let go of all things for the sake of the passionate pursuit of God's heart? Where do you think the pleasure in being a Christian is found? In the way of upholding what is and the way things are? Or in laying everything down and counting it as no better than rubbish, should anything get in the way of really knowing Christ and cooperating with the Holy Spirit in the building up of His Church? I pray we may all become so captivated by Christ Jesus, so consumed with passion for Him, desire for His glory alone, that we pick up the banner of genuine unity and plant it firmly in our own hearts and churches. May it be the clarion call of all believers to align themselves with the heart cry of Jesus, 'that they may be one as we are' (John 17:11).

The delights of welcoming, of forgiving, of blessing, of serving and building together in the glorious purpose of God, will far

Pleasure in One Another

outweigh the challenges and pain of getting there. It will open fresh visions of heaven, and heaven on earth.

Sceptical? I invite you to try it.

'I have no greater joy', says John, 'than to hear that my children are walking in the truth' (3 John 4). What does it feel like when you hear of a church that is enjoying greater demonstrations of God's blessing and favour than yours? The youth group is growing in numbers, the pastor has been on TV. The media picks up the dramatic events. What does it do to your heart? Are you like John? I confess I get very excited. I rejoice at what God is doing. Then I stamp my foot and shout to God, 'When is it going to rain on my patch?'

Dear Christian, you have an obligation in God to love me, to honour me, to lay down your life for me. Based exclusively in the indwelling Holy Spirit. As I also do to you. It is never primarily based on beliefs or doctrine or theology. Jesus never said have perfect theology, but love as I love you.

'Love one another deeply, from the heart' (1 Peter 1:22); 'Above all, love each other deeply, because love covers over a multitude of sins … so that in all things God may be praised through Jesus Christ. To him be the glory and the power for ever and ever. Amen' (1 Peter 4:8–11).

- How well do you know the Christians in your neighbourhood who attend a different fellowship?
- Do you support any schemes where you live that seek to encourage closer love and fellowship among believers?
- Could you initiate one?

Chapter 6
Displeasure

It would be wrong for me to ignore the scriptures which speak of God's displeasure.

As in all our human relationships, we are aware of attitudes and behaviours which result in pain and distress, so in the spiritual we find the same things bring distress to God's heart.

Contrary to what many may think, God takes no pleasure in the death of the wicked. His desire is that they turn from wickedness and live. He has no delight in the consequences that accompany their sin. Rather He delights to call them to Himself that they may enjoy the blessings of His love. God's mercy triumphs over judgement, and His constant cry is: 'Why will you die … ? … I take no pleasure in the death of anyone … Repent and live!' (Ezekiel 18:32).

God is the Author of life. He is the Giver and Sustainer of life. Death is that separation from the blissful reality of His lovely presence. He finds no pleasure in such separation. He has never given anyone life so that they can turn from Him into death. His character is alien to such thinking. Jesus came 'to seek and to save' that which was lost (see Luke 19:10). I am included in that, and so is everyone.

God takes no pleasure in evil. The evil acts of men are an abhorrence to His holiness. The psalmists lament, more than once, over the seeming 'blessing' under which evil men enjoy long life, wealth and comfort. We know that God will not be mocked and that such behaviour will have its ultimate reward. Can the enticing, although fleeting, comforts and securities of this life hold attraction to a true child of God? We all want more or greater when it comes to financial ease, health, a strong family life and relationships. All of this is normal and right, unless any of it becomes bigger than God in our affections. How many times do we begin trading eternal treasures for dust and ashes? Eternal life in Christ is a far greater reality than anything we can experience of this world. Yes, as with the psalmist I lament the injustice and unfairness of the struggles of this life while others indifferently celebrate their wealth and comforts. But, at what price? There is an answer in the Psalms, where it tells us: 'When I tried to understand all this, it was oppressive to me till I entered the sanctuary of God; then I understood their final destiny. ... Whom have I in heaven but you? And earth has nothing I desire besides you' (Psalm 73:16–17,25, NIV 1984). I remember at a gathering this scripture was mentioned, in song. As we discussed it, one member commented that it was not true for them. This person deeply desired a spouse to make their life complete. They openly confessed that God was not enough. There are so many challenging issues such as this that we have to grapple with in this life. God promises us His glorious pleasures as we seek and follow Him, as we rest in who He is and adore Him. Through faith we can embrace His promises thereby releasing His pleasure afresh in us.

Yes, the evil acts of men bring them prosperity. It is confusing, unfair and unjust, as we see it. But when we choose to move into the secret place with God, when we join our heart and will with His, then we have an opportunity to understand something of His perfect ways. There is a reminder, afresh, of just how satisfying He is above all things. We can come to understand just

Displeasure

how much more He is in comparison to everything else in life – 'earth has nothing I desire besides you.' Holding strongly to God, knowing Him to be love and to never fail, is our refuge in the middle of all the things we see and of which we are often victims, through the ungodliness of men. I pray we may all have a heart and the faith to see and to know as the psalmist does.

Our world appears to be getting smaller. News is more rapidly sent across the nations. Social media frequently sends images of incidents as they happen. The sheer volume of all this information can cause us to think that everything is getting worse and more hopeless. I do not believe this is so. In the middle of it all, the good news still changes lives, frees the captives and releases the kingdom of God into countless situations. I believe the darkness is getting darker, for sure, but not increasing. The Bible speaks of darkness covering the earth and deep darkness, the peoples (see Isaiah 60:2). If it is covering the earth, it cannot increase. The darkness gets darker. But the sinful expressions of what is in the heart of unregenerate man are as they have always been. It is the proliferation of news information which creates this picture of global chaos and fear. We are seeing and hearing of atrocities that at one time never reached our conscience. We should be thankful that things once hidden are being revealed, unpalatable as so much of it is. Our God has not abdicated! The Scriptures tell us these things will happen.

Nearly 2,000 years ago, Paul wrote about how and why God would give men over to their ungodly desires and inclinations. In the first chapter of Romans we read that though people know about God through what is revealed in creation, they choose to worship what they can see rather than the One who created it all. We live in a world of mass idolatry and false religions. One result of this is the spreading manifestation of sexual depravity which follows such idolatry. It has always been so, but in our society among earlier generations was kept behind locked doors, or ignored because of social sensitivities. Both men and women consumed with unnatural sexual desire towards one another... God takes no pleasure in this. I believe we will increasingly see God's hand of favour lift off our nations and churches for our capitulation and acceptance and even celebration of such practices.

Furthermore, Paul writes about the ongoing consequences of people turning their backs on God. In today's language, God says: 'OK, if that is what you want, get on with it.' The list is quite shocking and can be found in news bulletins every day: Every kind of wickedness, evil, greed, gossip, slanderers, God-haters, insolent, arrogant, boastful, inventing ways of doing evil, disobedient to parents, 'senseless, faithless, heartless, ruthless' (NIV 1984). Even going so far as to approve, or take pleasure in those who do such things. What an unwholesome catalogue. The Bible tells us that those who take delight in wickedness stand condemned before God. Hard as it is to live surrounded by such unrighteousness, Jesus invites us to be salt and light in this world. Salt preserves and flavours. Light destroys darkness and gives sight. We are here in the middle of all this to be that light which shows the better way. To stand as true models and examples of what living for God really looks like.

'Let your light shine before others, that they may see your good deeds and glorify your Father in heaven' (Matthew 5:16).

To this end we have many encouragements in the Bible, as well as some warnings. As I highlight some of these, I want to emphasise what I believe is God's heart for us at all times. I sum it up in some words of John Eldredge's from his book *Desire*, namely 'dutiful roses are a contradiction in terms' (Nashville, TN: Thomas Nelson, 2012). I don't believe God wants our duty.

Displeasure

I believe He wants our desire. He wants everything we are and do to flow from His love within us. It was out of His love that He gave. It is to be out of our love for Him that we choose to walk in obedience and agreement with Him. In this way I can turn from wrong behaviour and embrace godly ways because of love, not fear or duty.

What I mean can be seen in the example of the Israelites while they followed Moses out of Egypt and towards the Promised Land. Let's make no mistake here, they had left Egypt behind. They were set free through the Passover Lamb and the witness of the blood. They had been baptised into Moses as their leader and 'saviour'. They had the cloud of the Presence of God and His protective fire. They fed on God's miraculous supply, drank from His miraculous river that flowed from the rock and ran alongside them through the desert. But strikingly as the parallel is with us as believers today, God was not pleased with most of them. And they never reached their permanent vocation. Instead their carcasses rotted in the wilderness. Oh yes, they were saved from Egypt, set free from the bondage of slavery, feeding daily on God's miraculous provision, but never reached their God-ordained habitation.

The Promised Land is not heaven, however you perceive that to be. There are no idolatrous giants in heaven, no battles to fight to rid heaven of evil men. No defeats and sinful failures for God's people. So, what has brought God's displeasure? Well we know from 1 Corinthians 10 that the people became entangled in idolatry, in sexual immorality and abusing God's grace in their criticism of the way He cared for them. They grumbled against God and against Moses. When they reached the border of the Land they turned from trusting God and walked away into disobedience. Yet, even in their disobedience God faithfully cared, protected, provided and guided them as, for forty years, the hot tears of heaven buried one after another who had faithlessly rejected God's promise of a land flowing with milk and honey. We have this example, and yes, because our loving heavenly Father is full of grace and faithfulness, He will be with us, as with them, should we decide the way is too hard, or the price too high, and settle for less than… Walking through this life in the desert of compromise, of an empty cry being stifled in the struggle to adapt in the forms of our particular expression of Christianity.

The Scriptures tell us that those who love pleasure will become poor (see Proverbs 21:17). Pleasure not only relates to the enticements of this life. It also means the self-centred contentment of choosing our own path. Poverty of spirit is the reward, no matter how spiritual I attempt to be or try to convince others I am.

God assures us that His truth, His ways, commands and purposes are not idle words. They are our life (see Deuteronomy 32:47)!

His displeasure is seen in the way His favour fails to touch the lives of those who choose to dictate their own Christian path. It is this pride which prevents His grace from blessing those lives with overflow and abundance. He loves to give. We have to be healthy to receive His grace. He resists the proud and gives grace to the humble (see James 4:6). The humble are those who know that without dependence on the Holy Spirit they are impotent in terms of faithfully loving and following Jesus. What displeases God, I believe, is the pain of watching His children in the pain of shallow experiences of God. Seeing the pain of knowing there is more, but not pressing in and through to embrace it. The pain of a heart that aches for God while settling for something other. It is in witnessing the pain we bring on ourselves through lack of true

Displeasure

faith and trust in Him and His all-embracing love.

What has happened to that first love?

'Remember those earlier days after you received the light, when you stood your ground in a great contest in the face of suffering. Sometimes you were publicly exposed to insults and persecution; at other times you stood side by side with those who were so treated. You sympathised with those in prison and joyfully accepted the confiscation of your property, because you knew that you yourselves has better and lasting possessions' (Hebrews 10:32–34, NIV 1984). You know you had better and lasting possessions! Does that still hold true? Have the struggles of life, the church disappointments, maybe the seduction of 'things' taken their toll on that strong belief in the all-sufficiency of Father God? Do not throw away your confidence, it will be richly rewarded. The God who captivated your heart at the beginning is the same unchanging God today. He is eternally unchanging and faithful. Circumstances change. The Rock of our salvation is secure, unmoving and safe. So in persevering, we are able to complete the purposes of God in our lives, and receive what He has promised. For, 'he who is coming will come and will not delay' (Hebrews 10:37). The righteous live by faith, but if we shrink back God will not be pleased with us (see Hebrews 10:38). Given that we all desire pleasure at all times, pursuing God whatever it takes most enables that desire to be realised.

Anything that invades your mind and heart bringing thoughts of hopelessness, of a God who cannot or will not 'come through' for you, is a lying, deceiving voice from the father of lies. God is God, all the time. If He was good yesterday, He is today and will be tomorrow. He cannot change. He has no pleasure in our unbelief, as He watches the pain and damage it inflicts on us when we operate out of it. *Abba* God tells us that His truth, once received and believed sets us free. Anything and everything that is not in accord with His truth is a lie, whatever it may look like. He offers His grace to empower us to choose to believe and stand in His truth.

Jesus speaks of this in the parable of the sower. He refers to the seed which falls among thorns, stating that 'as they go on their way they are choked by life's worries, riches and pleasures, and they do not mature' (Luke 8:14). These believers have God's life and truth in them, but because they allow the stuff of life to overwhelm and negate this life-giving truth of God's revelation to their hearts and minds, they remain in struggle and confusion, and failure. This then tends to multiply over time as successive situations refuse to bring God's answer and freedom, since doubt clouds their view. The wrong sort of pleasure fills their 'pleasure zone', more than the pleasures found in the heart of Father. It is the wrong sort of pleasure simply because it dethrones the pleasures which are freely available at the Father's right hand.

In the middle of this struggle and frequent sense of failure, I want to speak some words of hope and life. Weak love is still love. What do I mean by that? Simply that within all of this life stuff, its challenges and the pressures we feel, and especially when we fail, the truth that we really do love God is still true. Yes, it may be a love that is weak, sometimes barely recognisable as love, sometimes struggling to stay intact in our hearts and affections, but we do still really love God. This love, offered to Him, in all its paucity, is so eagerly seized on by Father God and cherished. We are all on this journey into the glorious beauty of the abundance of the lavishness of the pure, holy heart of God our Father. We are all at different stages and places on this journey. Immaturity is not sin, it is a stage in growth. Immaturity is not the same as rebellion. Rebellion is a wilful rejection of

Displeasure

God's truth and ways, so as to do what is desired. Immaturity is a place of not yet being and understanding who we really are in God and living out of that place while aspiring towards greater things in God. Rebellion is choosing my own way when I really know it is contrary to God's, and at that moment, do not care or find the strength in faith to defeat it. Immaturity is seen in a desire to please and follow God without truly knowing how, or finding the strength of faith to do it.

But, remember, God is never impressed with our excuses. We cannot dress rebellion in the garb of immaturity and think we can fool God. We read in Hebrews about believers who ought to be mature and showing others the right way to love and worship, yet are continuing to live on spiritual baby food. They have failed to grow up in the faith and knowledge of God. Interestingly, the foundation of the faith is a true spiritual understanding of repentance from dead works (man-made religion and its rules); of faith towards God; correct biblical instruction and practice about baptisms and the laying on of hands, plus the resurrection of the dead and eternal judgement. This is foundational, as Hebrews 6:1-2 makes clear. True understanding and Holy Spirit illumination is the beginning of the Christian walk. The author also tells us that we need God's permission to move forward into greater maturity. Unless we hunger and thirst for righteousness, we will not be filled.

Paul speaks to the Corinthians about their immaturity and carnality. Carnal means 'of the flesh'. It encourages and responds to the natural sensations and senses, the feelings and desires of the flesh nature. This is enmity towards God. As believers, the flesh nature is put to death through Jesus. Through the enabling of the Holy Spirit we are able to choose and exercise control over the carnal mind and find the means to walk in obedience in the Spirit.

The carnality he highlights is the fledgling 'denominationalism' which is sprouting within the Corinthian community of believers. Read again in chapters 1 and 3 of 1 Corinthians and see what God says about divisions and party spirit. What was happening was that some people were lining themselves up alongside certain leaders. 'I'm of Paul', 'I'm of Apollos' and such-like. Some even used Jesus for the same party spirit. The response? 'Is Christ divided? Was Paul crucified for you? Were you baptised in the name of Paul?' There are over 30,000 different denominations in the worldwide Church. I am convinced that is more than 30,000 too many! All of them formed because of a carnal mind. What has happened has been that spiritual revelation has been rejected by 'established' churches, causing those with the revelation to gather together round that revelation. Often this has meant turning from the norms and forms of the day. How much this has been Holy Spirit-led is open to every man's opinion. What I do know is that God is a God of unity. He only separates when He is causing those who are faithful to leave that which does not honour and follow Him.

Some have been the result of different ideas about how to 'do church'. We are actually called to 'be Church' not 'do church'. In the same way we can never 'go to church' since we are Church. Obviously we meet together but that is really congregating together. Buildings are not churches. They are buildings with the purpose of keeping the weather off the Church, as I mentioned earlier, and enabling its congregating.

Most of what is meant by how we 'do church' relates to the way our Sunday gatherings are conducted. I know from experience that we have created many ways to 'do church'. I grew up with and, as a young pastor, initially followed the same form, the 'hymn sandwich'. (Hymn, prayer, hymn, bible reading, hymn,

Displeasure

sermon, hymn, go home.) I've used the Prayer Book, I've known 'bells and smells', I've known sitting in silence and 'happy clappy'. And so on. I've crossed various denominational thresholds. My simple observation is that I find so little in Scripture, if anything, to justify much of this. I hear comments such as 'I like the quiet traditional way' or 'I like the modern, more noisy way', 'I like spontaneous', 'I like structure where we always know what is coming', and similar words we have probably all used at some time or other.

But is this the right attitude? I believe that at its heart, worship has nothing to do with what 'I' like. Worship is fully centred on God. It is all about Him. It is that which gives Him pleasure. It is not about my favourite hymns, not about whether I like that tune, or how the musicians are dressed. My well-being and comfort are very secondary to what God is seeking. Jesus tells us that the Father is looking for true worshippers who will worship Him in Spirit and truth. God is Spirit and those who worship Him must worship in Spirit and truth (see John 4:23–24). This tells me that true worship is in the spirit and in the truth. That means that true worship, which means to 'draw near to kiss the feet' is all focused on God. The 'truth' is about the condition of the heart in all we say and do, as well as saying and doing what is right in God's sight. The 'spirit' is allowing and enabling the Holy Spirit to inspire, direct and empower all we do and say. I see no room for 'me' in that. I also believe that the joyful outcome of such true worship is the great sense of satisfaction we get from our devotion to our beautiful Saviour and King. I will sing this song in that tune I don't like, because it will bless God's heart. I will give myself fully to Him in this offering of praise and worship because it gives Him pleasure. In all this I find that I enjoy and see the value of all that such worship involves, and it pleases me also. The way we 'do church' has one simple focus, namely, that which pleases God.

To put a human face on it, I wonder, does God go home full and satisfied from His visit to our worship times?

The *ecclesia*, the called-out and separated to God community of born-again lovers and followers of Jesus, is the Church He said He would build. Turn the pages of the Bible and we quickly encounter Pentecost. It was during this annual Jewish festival that the outpouring of Holy Spirit, whose *'dunamis'* power propelled the disciples into church life and ministry, began the fulfilment of Jesus' words. The DNA of the Church Jesus is building, according to Scripture, is seen in the fullness and overflow of Holy Spirit in each believer, creating local community, which demonstrates the gospel through spiritual gifts, signs, wonders and miracles.

Jesus said that 'if you are offering your gift at the altar and there remember that your brother has something against you, leave your gift there in front of the altar. First go and be reconciled to your brother: then come and offer your gift' (Matthew 5:23–24, NIV 1984). That word 'something' cannot exclude the denominational and theological differences which keep carriers of Holy Spirit from the fullness of unity in Jesus through the Holy Spirit. With such offerings, God is not pleased. Reading Malachi chapter 1 gives cause to pause and reflect. God pleads for the doors of the sanctuary to be slammed shut to keep worshippers out rather than have unacceptable, less than perfect sacrifices of praise presented to Him. He thunders that we would not show such lack of diligence and respect towards an employer, so why do it to Him? 'I am not pleased with you,' says the Lord (1:10). Father God is never impressed with excuses, no matter how legitimate they seem. How do we justify our denominations and the way we 'do church'? Are we able to line them up with

Displeasure

what the Scriptures reveal and teach us?

God's displeasure is seen also in such issues as the way we treat the poor and marginalised. I know the Christian community excels in this, across the nation, in so many ways. I thank God for that. But to show indifference at any time makes our prayers and collective times of worship things that are unacceptable and bring God no joy. Isaiah chapter 58 highlights this. I find it a constant invitation (the word I prefer to the word 'challenge') that there are probably enough empty bedrooms in the homes of Christians, including my own, to clear the streets of the homeless in this country. Sometimes the invitations to follow Jesus dig very deeply into the heart, lifestyle and comfort.

Although God loves us perfectly, persistently and passionately, He still will not tolerate anything that draws us away from Him in any way. Such things dethrone Him in our affections. That damages our life in Him and undermines the joy and peace which are ours in Christ Jesus. As a youth I was a fanatical football supporter. Saturday afternoons would find me standing on the terraces cheering on my team. This included joining in the abuse of the opposition and language which was anything but righteous. But you had to join in, that is how things were. I would shout myself hoarse. Therein lay my invitation to give everything to God. I sang in the church choir on Sunday evenings. Trying to sing with no voice is not easy, nor pleasant on the ears. What was I to do? Eventually my decision was made. I love God much more than football. I love to sing about Him much more than sing of my team. Thus, for me, it was a no-brainer. The visits to the football ground stopped. I could not attend in silence. Not possible. The only thing I could honestly do before my God and King was to separate myself from that which prevented me giving my all and my best to, and for, Him. I mention this to illustrate

The Pursuit of Pleasure

how sometimes the 'little foxes' can spoil the vines (Song of Songs 2:15). It was not wrong to attend the football match. Not wrong to shout and sing, apart from the obscenities, of course! It was simply the accumulative effect on my walk with Jesus. I am as aware today, as then, for the need to keep praying for revelation and discernment about the little things of life. I do not want to be less than all for God in every way.

The Bible instructs us not to get drunk. Being drunk in the Spirit, as the disciples were accused of being at Pentecost, is good and something to be pursued. Yet I have lost count over the years of the number of times someone has skipped meeting together to worship on a Sunday morning because of the after-effects of the night before. Or because of an unnecessarily late night. I am not being judgemental here, simply stating it like it is. It is all about the heart attitude before God. It is about the desire for Him above everything else. Ezekiel and Hosea both speak of God's displeasure at the adulterous idolatry which shows the lack of passionate desire for Him when confronted with the enticements of this world (Ezekiel 16, Hosea 9).

Pornography is a serious, destructive prison for so many Christians. My own experience and ministry as well as comment pages suggest a high proportion is not an exaggeration. Saturday night in front of the TV or computer then Sunday morning in the pulpit or pew. I've been there, I know what it is like. I know what devastation it causes. We turn up on Sunday mornings wearing our Sunday face hoping to convince everyone that we have it all together in our lives. Of course, God is never convinced by this show. I pray that our fellowships will grow in love, honour, respect and safety to the point where this evil can be mentioned and dealt with without accusation or judgement. Where people can make themselves vulnerable and receive the

Displeasure

healing and freedom for which Jesus gave His life. Then there will be great joy in the heart of the Father as we bring acceptable sacrifices of praise. Obviously for churches to become healthy Spirit-filled communities, they need godly Spirit-filled overseers. God has some strong words for those who do not fulfil this mandate. Through Jeremiah He speaks of those 'shepherds' who do not care properly for the sheep. They turn His vineyard into a desolate wasteland (Jeremiah 12:10–11). Jesus calls the religious leaders of His day 'blind guides'. There are various passages which enforce this view and show God's sorrow at such behaviour.

Church leaders, whatever title is used to delineate their function, have a most awesome privilege and responsibility before God. The responsibility to feed and care for the people. Feeding means meaningful, relevant, understandable spiritual truth that sets people free. It means preaching the good news of forgiveness and salvation in Jesus alone, by grace through faith in God's revealed word seen in Jesus. It means calling people into a deep, meaningful relationship with the Father in the Holy Spirit. It means applying God's truth to the everyday situations of life. Inspiring people to trust God first, whatever it looks like round about. It means no compromise with the utterly ungodly 'political correctness' of the days in which we live which constantly condemns God's truth as well as common sense. The teaching of universalism, multifaith acceptability, new age godless philosophies, and self-help works salvation, have no place within what is God's *ecclesia*. Such deceptions cause desolation to God's beautiful vineyard. As are those who deny the reality of the gifts of the Holy Spirit and substitute cerebral religion for spiritual reality and relationship with God.

Ezekiel chapter 34 is a scathing denouncement on those so-called shepherds who look out for themselves, their career prospects, their unavailability, their reputations and fame at the cost of true spiritual ministry to those under their care. I have been in meetings with members of the clergy who have no idea about a living relationship with God; people who do not believe in the reality of the physical birth, life, death and resurrection of Jesus. Yet they see themselves as shepherds of God's flock. Such people leave the sheep uncertain, fearful, spiritually empty, and vulnerable to whatever ideas are the flavour of the month. Then there are some who tickle the ears of their listeners speaking platitudes which they know their listeners want to hear. Here we have a toxic cocktail of unrighteousness which is causing 'Church' to collapse and be given over to all sorts of contemporary pick-and-mix religion, deprived of truth and life.

Not comfortable reading, and not a scenario which gladdens the heart of God. Sadly I see this everywhere I look within what is called Christianity. It is far too serious to ignore. Far too serious to be offended about. The generation of 'not yet Christians' among whom we live are sliding indifferently into an eternity separated from the grace and lovely Presence of God. There are people in many churches who are not Christian while believing they are. There are many people outside of churches who are Christians, but are turned away by what they see, hear and experience. Both situations are wrong. They are contrary to God's purposes for His Church, the *ecclesia*. He finds no pleasure in this.

The good news is that we do not have to go down these paths. Although I have spoken about church leaders, every individual believer is personally responsible for the state of their heart and life in God. We all have the same Holy Spirit. We all have the same power which raised Jesus from the dead. We all have the same Bible. We all have the same twenty-four hours in every day. My faith is in God, not in His people, however experienced or clever

Displeasure

they may be. He is my salvation. He is my glory and the lifter of my head. His is the power for me to turn from temptation. His is the love to draw me deeper into Him and His truth. We can all say 'yes' to God, knowing His Spirit in us is greater than everything opposing us. He declares it to be; I choose to believe Him – do you? Obviously there is real purpose and value for all believers in the ministry gifts God has lavished on His Church. We have a responsibility to honour, bless, support and receive the truth brought to our lives through them. This is part of my own responsibility before God. Making such a commitment before God leads me into the pleasures of eternal joy to be found in Him.

Out of passionate love for God I urge that we turn from everything which displeases Him to embrace the good gifts He desires us to receive, enjoy and live in.

I do not believe any true lover and follower of Jesus really wants to turn from Him, to do their own thing, to despise His grace, yet we so easily find ourselves in that place. Thank God for His grace. Without it, where would we be?

- In examining your own life, do you see things that displease God?
- What steps can you take to change such things?
- Does 'church' as you know it truly measure up to the biblical picture?

Chapter 7
Pleasure in the Father

This is something I came to understand many years after I first came to know Jesus. From the beginning I was blessed to know that God was my heavenly Father. I have been enjoying knowing that truth all these years. But I have found that that is not the same as actually enjoying Him for who He is. I want to explore this wonderful consciousness a little with you.

So, pleasure in the Father? How can this be? Surely God is to be held in awe? The Bible teaches us that. 'The fear of the LORD is the beginning of wisdom' (Psalm 111:10). God is holy. He is Almighty. Most certainly not just like us. Should I be writing about pleasure in the Father? Firstly, the fear of the Lord is not about being scared. For too long too many Christians have been held by the deception that God, who is love, who is always good, is someone to be scared of. Not at all. The fear spoken of here relates to reverence, honour and respect. It speaks of acknowledging that God is God, and of living accordingly. I tell the truth, not because I am scared God will 'catch me out' and punish me in some way, but because I love Him and delight in His ways which bring me pleasure and elevate Him even more to my understanding. Since I am a living, walking advertisement for what the gospel looks like and means to this generation, I want to live a life that presents God in a good, positive, loving way. I see this as living in awe of God.

Another stumbling block to pleasure with God is a fear of

emotion. This fear still prevails among Christians, especially when the more expressive forms of worship and preaching are witnessed. There seems to be a latent fear of emotionalism and of people getting carried away in the moment. This is often perceived to produce a shallow form of faith. But God is very emotional. And He made us in His image and declared that everything He had made is good, as we see in the book of Genesis. We are all emotional beings, so why relate to God only on a cerebral level?

The two disciples walking with Jesus on the Emmaus road spoke of how their hearts burned within them as He walked and spoke with them (see Luke 24). If that is not emotional, I don't know what is. God is very emotional. He laughs (Psalm 2). He gets angry (Exodus 4:14). He longs for relationship with us (Jeremiah 3:19; Hosea 2:16). He weeps (John 11:35). Why respond and trust emotions in human relationships, yet distrust them with God? Do not we all find it easy to tell our loved ones that we love them? And then to behave in ways that show that love? We speak lovingly to spouses, children and friends. We are happy and comfortable to show our emotions. We buy gifts and treats to re-enforce the affection in which we hold one another. The psalmist speaks of his heart and his flesh crying out for God (Psalm 84:2). Our heart is the seat of our emotions. We weep in our pain and are comforted that God knows what we are going through. He is held by our emotional outburst and overflow and collects out tears in a bottle (Psalm 56:8, KJV). But how many of us feel comfortable laughing in His presence, as in a worship meeting? It seems OK to weep, but not to laugh. What is behind this attitude, I wonder. How powerful is the love of God in and to you?

The idea that God has separated Himself because He is so much 'other' than we are, to the point that He cannot be enjoyed, is contrary to the teaching of the Bible from Genesis to Revelation. We cannot claim to truly love God without having a relationship with Him. If that relationship is no more than duty, if it is simply a mental agreement that God is, then it is not the relationship Jesus died to bring us into. The Holy Spirit empowers us to call God '*Abba*, Father' (Romans 8:15). *Abba* means 'daddy'. It is a term of endearment and affection. An expression of close relationship. The word on the lips of a child, happy, secure, enjoying knowing who its daddy is and comforted in that knowing. There is no hint of a Victorian disciplinarian who is removed from emotional contact, and believed that children should be seen and not heard.

Jesus spoke of His joy being in us, making our joy complete (see John 15:11). The psalmist speaks of joy and eternal pleasure in the Presence of God (see Psalm 16:11). Yes, pleasure in the Father is the birthright of every truly born again child of God. 'Whom have I in heaven but you? And earth has nothing I desire besides You' (Psalm 73:25). The Hebrew words emphasise pleasure. The psalmist is stating that there is nothing that gives as much pleasure to him as being a child of God. The birth of a child, the song of a bird, the delicate, fragile beauty of a flower, the majesty of mountains, the music of Bach or Beethoven, all so full of delight and deep satisfying pleasure. Our Father God throws out this invitation: 'You can desire Me more than all this, if you want to.'

Do you want to? Does your heart ever long for a deeper knowing of God? A desire to be closer, more in love with Jesus, an unrelenting sense that there has to be more than what it is like right now? Maybe you have tried all the conferences, read the books, listened to the teaching programmes, none of which is wrong, but the secret is this – when our hearts truly yearn for God, He has promised to fill and to overflow. It is not really a secret. It is written clearly across the pages of Scripture. 'If you are thirsty, come to me and drink!' (John 7:37, CEV). 'Blessed are those who hunger and thirst for righteousness, for they will be filled' (Matthew 5:6). When we set our hearts to know Him, He will be found by us. He delights to hide sufficiently to create and increase heart hunger for Him. Then He puts Himself right in front of us so that we find Him. Truly knowing God comes from hunger. The conferences, books and teaching materials are so often a means to realising this deep heart hunger. I am so thankful for the times when He has impacted me through these things.

Do you have such a desire for God to so overwhelm you, spirit, soul and body, that He becomes the greatest desire and pleasure of your whole life? Have you told God this? Have the words ever passed your lips? Does your life tell Him of your desire?

Let me quote a few lines from an email I recently received from Charley, a young woman I know, who sent this while away from home, learning more of God and serving him in a foreign country. I have her permission to include this.

> Last time I tried to paint I couldn't put my brush to the canvas as I was weeping as God was giving me revelation of His love. I was praising with my roommates and saying, 'Jesus show me Your face, I want to see Your face.' Then it hit me, He has given me everything. I would love to see His face, but what a privilege it is that I know His name. If that is all I ever have then that is more than enough. I know my Saviour's name. I know my Lover's name. Wave after wave of this revelation and I was on my knees, weeping. Wow! So He keeps encountering me in ways I've never known before, and there is so much more of Him. It is all just a waste if I don't have more of Him.

Pleasure in the Father

'It is all just a waste if I don't have more of Him.' This was written by someone who has just brought a group of teenagers to faith in Jesus; who has seen some remarkable miracles of healing. These things are not a 'waste', indeed they are of eternal value. But, in comparison to knowing and experiencing Jesus, to growing in passion and abandonment to Him, it all fades into shadows. It is not primarily about the doing, it is all about the knowing. In the words of Jesus: 'Many will say to me on that day, "Lord, Lord, did we not prophesy in your name and in your name drive out demons and … perform many miracles?" Then I will tell them plainly, "I never knew you. Away from me, you evildoers!"' (Matthew 7:22–23). These people believed that doing things for God was what God wanted of them. They believed it showed their devotion. Yet they missed the real truth of the matter which is that God desires our love, our hearts. Everything else flows from that. Jesus said, 'Go away. I've never known you.' They had no relationship with God, only a life of servitude. This despite the miraculous they testified to. I think of Mary who sat at Jesus' feet, enthralled by His words and Presence, while Martha was busy and distracted. Martha was doing good things, but missing the better and greater part, which was what Mary had found (see Luke 10:38–42).

In Isaiah we read, 'I delight greatly in the LORD; my soul rejoices in my God' (61:10). To 'delight greatly' also means to 'enjoy'. To 'rejoice in my God' can also be translated 'to leap and be joyful'. Therefore, we can read these words as saying, 'I greatly enjoy the Lord. My innermost being leaps about joyfully in my God.' We know the Scriptures teach us of the pleasure and joy to be found in God. Are you able to say this is your experience of Him? Do you want it to be your experience? Isaiah found something which all of us can know, as God is no respecter of persons. What the prophet discovered, we too may find and experience. If you want to get closer to Jesus, there is nothing that can stand in your way.

'They feast in the abundance of your house; you give them drink from your river of delights. For with you is the fountain of life; in your light we see light' (Psalm 36:8–9). Father God is offering a feast; why be satisfied with a snack? Maybe you have always got by on snacks, and a snack from God is full of good, life-giving sustenance. So, how much more is the feast? And it *is* a feast. A feast of abundance. This is an 'eat all you can desire, it never diminishes' sort of feast. Right now I pray that God will stir up in all of us a deeper hunger for Him. A holy dissatisfaction with the way things are. A longing for them to become so much more.

'Come and drink from My delightful river of life' is the invitation. Jesus cried out, 'If anyone is thirsty, let him come to me and drink. Whoever believes in me, as the Scripture has said, streams of living water will flow from within him.' By this he meant the Spirit, whom those who believed in him were later to receive. Up to that time the Spirit had not been given, since Jesus had not yet been glorified' (John 7:37–39, NIV 1984). I cannot overstate the crucial importance and impact of the Holy Spirit. Jesus Himself declared that without Holy Spirit, He was impotent. 'The Son can do nothing by himself', He said (John 5:19). How much more you and me?

It is so important to get to know the Holy Spirit intimately. To learn to recognise His Presence and promptings. To learn to live out of the overflow of His fullness. To learn not to strive, but rather to rest and choose to cooperate with Him. Only then will this delightful river of life begin to be a reality. Of course, it takes time to get to know someone and begin to recognise their ways.

Pleasure in the Father

God has all the time in the world. He simply waits for us to want Him. Jesus said: '*If* anyone is thirsty' (emphasis mine). Such a tiny word, such a weight of importance.

While watching the film *Compelled by Love* (2014), the story of Rolland and Heidi Baker, I was struck by a comment that Rolland made. He and Heidi have devoted their lives to God and His service. This has taken them into various situations around the world – in China, London and Mozambique as well as surrounding nations. Their days are spent feeding, loving, teaching, saving and healing countless broken lives and bodies. They travel many thousands of miles every year in obedience to God to give away what He has poured into them. Yet Rolland said that his only purpose in life is to get closer to Jesus. What I believe we can discover for ourselves, more than anything else is this – the closer we come to Jesus, the deeper our devotion, the greater our passion, so His beauty and nature grows in us. And so 'the things of earth will grow strangely dim' (from 'Turn Your Eyes Upon Jesus', Helen Howarth Lemmel, 1863–1961). From this everything we do at His instigation becomes more fruitful, more kingdom-effective. It is never a case of either/or, rather, it is both/and. I have heard many times that the Church needs 'Marthas'. But if everyone is 'in church' praying, who is going to feed the hungry, clothe the naked, care for the sick and evangelise the lost? God has never demanded our busyness. His command is to believe in His Son, Jesus Christ, and to love one another (see 1 John 3:23). We read that Jesus chose the disciples 'that they *might be with him*, and that he might send them out to preach' (Mark 3:14, italics mine). He sought their company and friendship first. He longed for relationship before anointing them for ministry.

What constantly stops me in my tracks, holds me in awe and

wonder, grips my heart and mind in amazement, is this, that God actually loves me. He likes me. He desires my company. He wants to be in everything of my life. He wants to walk in the park with me. He wants to stand in the supermarket queue with me, to sit on the couch and watch TV with me, to be in every conversation and action with my wife and family. He wants to share my pleasures and pains.

He is the One who said, 'Never will I leave you; never will I forsake you' (Hebrews 13:5). So while I am chatting and eating with friends, He is there. In the workplace, He is there. He is also there when I pray and meet with other worshippers to celebrate and adore Him. We do not leave God behind when we exit the building.

The greater the intimacy, the more intense the passion. The more intense the passion, the greater the pursuit of the prize.

Paul puts it this way, 'whatever was to my profit I now consider loss for the sake of Christ. What is more, I consider everything a loss compared to the surpassing greatness of knowing Christ Jesus my Lord, for whose sake I have lost all things. I consider them rubbish, that I may gain Christ and be found in Him … I want to know Christ' (Philippians 3:7–10, NIV 1984).

'For to me, to live is Christ, and to die is gain' (Philippians 1:21). Oh for a devotion, a love which transcends all else, just to know Jesus. To see Him in His glory and beauty. These are difficult words for our consumerist age. Comfort, security and 'stuff' so easily strangle the deep desires for Jesus. How am I to find this love which transcends all else? How well do I know God? I don't mean know about God. I mean to truly know Him relationally. It takes an act of the will. It takes time. The pressures of time are so strong these days, yet somehow we all find the time to do the things we want to do.

Pleasure in the Father

Isaiah speaks of there being joy in God's house of prayer (see Isaiah 56:7). Is prayer seen as a duty? As a chore? A drudge? Or is it time embraced to share your heart with your loving Father and to listen to His love songs for you?

In the Psalms we read that God's word is a delight. 'How sweet are your words to my taste', 'Oh, how I love your law! I meditate on it *all day long*' (Psalm 119:103,97, emphasis mine). Meditating all day long includes how we choose to respond to situations we face based on what the Scriptures teach. Our responses reflect our knowledge, how we embrace God's word, and our faith in it. To act against His teaching shows our disregard for God and His truth. Yes, we can all react in ways we regret and know to be wrong. Then we simply repent, confess and get it put right, making a determination to change. I am referring here to wilful, careless indifference to God's word. Something that speaks loudly and clearly of a lack of love for Him. The more we choose to learn of Him and allow the Holy Spirit to reveal the character and nature of God to us, the more likely we are to grow in love and wonder.

We read of how the early Church met together every day to worship, pray and eat. Not only did they do this, but they devoted themselves to this community lifestyle. We also see that they were of one heart and mind, sharing all they had with each other, so that no one was in need. Jesus said that the love we have for Him will be seen in the love we have for one another. I know twenty-first century life gets in the way, but is it really beyond believers today to live in such community lifestyle without resorting to a monastic expression? I honestly believe it is, even in families where there is an unbelieving spouse or children. I cry to God for revelation to highlight the pathway that will bring about such a social transformation in our communities. Then the world will

The Pursuit of Pleasure

know we are His disciples, through the power of love flowing in sacrificial, joy-filled honouring of one another.

In my book *Feasting on the Father*, I ask a question with which the Father challenged me. He said, 'Would you lay down your life for the Christians in the church you do not attend?' I still wrestle with that question. I now know it is not based on whether I know the people. It is based on my choice to love the Lord my God will all my heart, soul, mind and strength. That will cause me to love my neighbour as myself. It is not only an invitation from God, it is also a promise. When I am so in love with God that He becomes the total focus of my life, the purpose of my waking in the morning, and using my energy to please Him, by the worship of my life, so I will find myself loving those around me. I won't be able to help myself! And this pleases the Father.

Does this make sense? I know it does to me, but I confess to struggling to put into words what is so strong in my heart. The more glorious God becomes to us, the more beautiful, overwhelming and stunning, the more captivated we become by the wonder of His unrelenting, fathomless love, the more naturally will we reflect His nature and character. The more like Jesus we will become and the more the people around us will encounter Jesus.

Prayer, worship, the Bible, meeting with other believers, all take on a glory which is the Presence and satisfying goodness of our loving Father God. Christian faith can be summed up in this, I believe. I receive the love of God and return love to Him with everything I am and have, coming from that unfathomable, perfect love that He has lavished on me. And everything else proceeds out of that. How can we not be completely taken up by Him, as we come to know Him, and understand His love for us?

This amazing Creator God so loves me that He came to this

earth, as a man, to willingly give His life to make it possible for me to be freed from sin and become part of His new creation family. All I have had to do is acknowledge the wrong, the imperfection in me (sin), turn away from it (repent) and, by faith, receive not only God's forgiveness, but also His justification. What does that mean? It is basically a legal term which makes the declaration that I am not guilty. When Jesus took my sin onto Himself and took it to the grave, I was declared to be not guilty. Because of Jesus, God now sees me 'just-as-if-I'd' never sinned. I am holy and blameless in His sight (Ephesians 1:4). This is something of the enormity of God's love for us, for you. As the Scriptures declare, we love Him because He first loved us.

Paul speaks of having been crucified with Christ (Galatians 2:20), of being buried with Him in baptism (Romans 6:4), and of being united with Him in His resurrection (Romans 6:5). In this way we become 'new creations' (2 Corinthians 5:17) in Christ Jesus, through the Holy Spirit. We are now citizens of the kingdom of God. Taken from darkness to light. Everything is new. Especially the affections of our heart.

We have a new heart, made new in the Spirit. We are made in the image of God. God is love, therefore we are love. God is Spirit, we are Spirit. We are not human beings trying to live a spiritual life, we are actually spiritual beings living in a fallen flesh. At our core we are spiritual beings, because God is Spirit. There is a man in heaven, Jesus, the perfect Spiritual Man Being. The One and Only Mediator between God and humanity. He is perfect man. Totally at one, with and in the Father, as a man. This is, legally, what we are before God. And what we will ultimately be in our experiential relationship with the Father. For when we see Him, we shall be like Him (see 1 John 3:2). Throughout His earthly life, Jesus lived, a man, daily full to overflowing with Holy Spirit. He chose moment by moment, as a man, to submit Himself, fully, to the will (pleasure) and purposes of the Father. He overcame every temptation that we encounter, through this Spirit-filled yielded life. He did this as a man. Not 'as God', I believe, but as a man. He chose to subjugate His 'God-ness' to His humanity so that He might be fully a man in full Spirit-filled fellowship and submission to the Father. On what other grounds could He tell His disciples that they would do the works that He did, and greater works (John 14:12), if He had to be 'as God' to do them? After faithfully following the path to the cross and the grave, He rose again to life. He is now sitting at the Father's side, a man. The firstborn of a whole new race of Spirit-born and filled new creation humans who share in His resurrection life. This is what He has brought us into.

The wonder of what God's love has brought us into highlights the life we have in the Holy Spirit. The phrase, 'I'm only human' no longer applies. We are spiritual beings with a dead sinful nature that constantly strives to subjugate us to the demands of the flesh: 'Count yourselves dead to sin but alive to God in Christ Jesus' (Romans 6:11). In the Holy Spirit we have the power of God to refuse to let sin reign, or have control, in our body with its feelings, desires and affections. Rather, we can choose to offer ourselves to God, as instruments of righteousness (see Romans 6:13), since we have (already) been brought from death to life. The words, 'the one who is in you is greater than the one who is in the world' (1 John 4:4) are a great encouragement. It is eternal truth that at any and every given moment we can engage with the grace of God which is sufficient for whatever need in which we find ourselves. This is God's truth for us. This is how Jesus lived, leaving us an example that we should follow in His steps.

Now, to come back with a 'yes, but…' is, in reality, looking for

Pleasure in the Father

an 'opt out', an excuse. Looking for a way to justify pampering to the flesh and 'dead' sinful nature. Further to this, the person I am is so much less than the person God has recreated me to be. In comparison to the life in the Spirit, the natural life, the life of the flesh, is garbage, as Paul found out (see Philippians 3:7–11). Does anyone truly want to trade the dynamic of life in Jesus, for 'the fleeting pleasures of sin', as Hebrews states (Hebrews 11:25)? How well we know that the 'wages', or reward and consequences, 'of sin is death' (Romans 6:23). Not only in ultimate judgement, but in the moment of failure and day to day death in our spirit which is experienced when we choose our own way. The trade is simple, shame for sonship. Ugliness for beauty. Fear for fellowship. All it demands is the willingness to press on, to persist in choosing God's way, even when we have missed the mark and failed. Faith and trust in His grace bring us to a place of peace, security and victorious living.

Some time ago, God spoke these words to me:

> I am passionately jealous for your whole heart. I cannot settle for less than all of you. My jealousy is aroused when I see you giving yourself to anything, or anyone, other than Me. I delight in every moment you give yourself to Me. I never despise any time we share together. It is always a joy to Me, yet My whole purpose for you is to be wholly Mine. I know your heart will never be at rest and peace until it is wholly Mine. So I am jealous for your love. I hate the lovers that take your heart away from Me. My jealousy burns strongly and I will not settle for less than all of your heart. A bride-to-be sets her whole heart and mind on her beloved. She anticipates her wedding day and thinks constantly about the day she will be fully joined to her beloved. No bride shares her heart with another. She willingly

separates herself from all former lovers. She does not entertain any thoughts of a lover other than her beloved bridegroom. She gladly chooses to separate herself from everything that distracts her from her beloved, from her wedding day. She gives herself, fully, to all the preparations for the great day. Her heart and mind are totally given over to everything needful for that day. She busies herself with preparations. Nothing else seems to occupy her mind. Even daily needs become secondary to her, as the day draws closer and closer. She has separated herself to achieve the goal of being fully ready, in every way, for the day of her marriage. Her mind is consumed with the joy and wonder of being fully joined, at one, with her beloved. It is all she thinks and talks about. All her energies are directed towards the day of consummation. This separation has taken place, almost without a wilful turning from. Something she has happily embraced and has become indifferent to everything else. Even food and sleep become of secondary importance, in the face of her delightful obsession, preparing for her bridegroom. So you, My beloved Bride, are to separate yourself from everything which could hinder your preparations for our Wedding Day. There is always a 'leaving'. Abraham left his home and family to enter into My purposes for him. The result? The nation which birthed your salvation. I left My home to gain you and take you to Myself. This separation is not a hard thing when you are so deliriously captivated by your Beloved. So, ask Me, and I will give you that passionate desire which will cause you to abandon everything to know Me and become fully mine.

Having daughters who are married, I know something of the picture presented here of a bride to be!

Pleasure in the Father

I live now with an understanding I never used to have. Some years ago I was held by God in the story of the sacrifice Abraham was prepared to make of his son Isaac. I could not move on from this passage of Scripture for many weeks. 'What are You wanting me to see?' I kept asking. One day, Father unpacked something for me. It may never impact anyone else, but it has transformed my walk with God. He said this: 'Abraham is not sacrificing his son. Christians who obey and follow Me are not sacrificing. Those believers who sacrifice are the ones who live content to "go to church" on Sunday morning, put their money in the box and that's it. They live their life content with being a Christian.' I responded that I did not understand, what are they sacrificing? His reply changed me forever. 'They are sacrificing My Presence and My favour. They are sacrificing the joy and fun of partnering with Me in seeing My kingdom come on earth as in heaven. They are sacrificing the buzz of healing the sick, setting the captives free and the indescribable pleasure of bringing the lost to know Me. They are sacrificing the deeper things of My Spirit and understanding the truths of Scripture. The fellowship of hearts joined across the nations in ministry, worship and prayer. They are choosing the comfortable, secure, trouble-free sort of Christian walk, where being nice, and socially acceptable, is more desirable than living in the dynamic of My Spirit.'

I know I cannot make anyone love God more than at present. I confess I do want to excite a desire for all to hunger and thirst after Him with greater resolve and intensity. Only the thirsty drink and only the hungry eat. And what pleasure that brings.

I conclude this chapter with some words from the journal of a very precious friend whom my wife and I love and value greatly, thanking God for bringing Teresa into our lives. A lady who has suffered physical disability from birth. (This is used with permission.)

The Pursuit of Pleasure

Lying awake during another sleepless night, I was writing, 'Father God, Holy, Mighty, Awesome Father God, Lord of all, King of life and peace, I love You. I worship You, my God and my Saviour. Thank You for being in my life.' Then I was overwhelmed by tiredness and complete exhaustion. I carried on writing, 'Father I am so tired, again, so completely exhausted, so completely empty as though there is none of me left. Actually it's rather a nice feeling. I don't have to pretend anything or perform in any way. I don't have to worry about what people think of me. In fact I don't even need to factor in or play a part in anything, then all that is left is You. How amazing is that? What more better way could there be? Lord, thank You for bringing me to this place of surrender. I love you so much. I think I have found or have realised what true freedom really is. It is the emptiness of me and the all of You.

'Precious Jesus, my Lord and King, how I love You. Oh how I love You. How I completely, absolutely and totally love You. It is all about You. You quite simply are everything. You are what holds everything together. You are the fabric of the universe. You are the universe! You are life itself. Life is You. Everything about life is Jesus. Everything, everything is about Jesus! It is all about Jesus. The sky; the sun; the stars; the moon; the oceans; the mountains; the valleys; the deserts; the birds; the animals; the insects; the very breath of life, is all about Jesus. All about Jesus, Jesus, Jesus, JESUS, the Author and Perfecter of our faith. The Alpha and Omega, the Beginning and the End.

'Lord I love You with every part of my being. Lord I am alive in You. I breathe because You breathe. I laugh because You laugh. I live because You live. I am alive because You live in me. How amazing is that! How awesome and incredible and glorious is that. How I love You Jesus.

Pleasure in the Father

'Suddenly, for this particular moment in time, life makes sense. As though it has all come full circle, this yearning within me has become satiated. For this particular moment I have suddenly found peace, complete, absolute and perfect peace. And it is glorious. I think I have glimpsed heaven, or what it means to be in heaven. It is complete and utter fulfilment of the soul. Complete and utter emptiness of me and the complete and utter glory of Jesus, and it is so, so, so, so, so good. Thank You Jesus. Amen.'

I am beginning to realise that, for me, it is only when 'I' completely switch off and shut down (for want of a better way of putting it) that Jesus becomes so real and so much more powerful and effective in my life. Maybe that is why God allows me to go with so little sleep. Because when I am so completely exhausted and spent, that is when He becomes so alive, and it is so glorious, so wonderful, so amazing, so real, so perfect, and makes such complete sense to me, that I am buoyed up in my spirit and feel able to take on the world. Even though, physically, I am a wreck. Jesus is so wonderful, so beautiful, so precious, so amazing, so glorious, so incredible so absolute. It seems that the further and deeper we go, the more there is to discover and be revealed. How will I ever cope!

- How real is your story about Jesus in your life?
- If you are anything like me, you will be energised and inspired by other people's experiences of God. How do you follow that up?
- What sort of Father do you perceive God to be to you?

Chapter 8
Treasure, Price and Value

Treasure is something highly valued, something to be acquired and prized. Usually, in this world, something locked away for safety. It is often something rare, recognised as of great price. It takes various forms. We treasure an experience because of the pleasure it gave. We love to recall such occasions, the reasons for this 'treasure time'. The people, the place, the outcome. I look at people who are, or who have been, a part of my life. I greatly value the impact they have made on me. I value the qualities I see in them. Qualities which inspire me to reach for that 'something more' which they reflect. We treasure gifts associated with our loved ones, or special occasions. We treasure memories which capture special moments in our lives. It is interesting that Jesus recognised the power we attribute to treasure: 'where your treasure is, there your heart will be also' are the words He spoke (Luke 12:34). He said this in the context of worrying about 'stuff'. Of putting our trust in the perishable, inconsistent 'treasure' of our possessions. He sets out this comparison: the Father, in His pleasure, delights to give us the kingdom. Therefore, free yourself from the dependant ownership of your possessions. This is because whatever holds your heart is the treasure of your life. It really becomes your god.

So many people, from Adam onwards, have made shipwreck of their lives in pursuit of the 'treasure' of power, knowledge, prestige, reputation, wealth, a man, a woman, and so much more.

The Pursuit of Pleasure

When Jesus speaks of having to 'hate' our family (see Luke 14:26) to be true followers of Him, I believe He is speaking of this type of attachment. What holds your heart is the most priceless treasure, the passion, that which motivates or drives your life. The character of God, as portrayed in Jesus, does not allow for a literal understanding of those words. They challenge us to see a comparative perspective. In comparison to my love for God, the love I have for my family seems more like hate, because it is so much less passionate and all-consuming. I am called to 'give up' my family, in the devotion of my heart, rather than deny or give up God. This is the depth of love He is inviting us to know and enjoy. In reality, if I make my family more important than God, then my family has become my god, an idol which cannot save or satisfy.

He is not demanding that a person leave their family unsupported and destitute as they follow Jesus to 'the ends of the earth' (Acts 1:8). But, in whatever situation you are in, God knows every intimate detail. Whatever your life is like, God knows all about it, and should He ask anything of you, He asks in the knowledge of what your life looks like.

He calls us to establish heavenly treasure. This is done by giving away the love He pours into us; also by treating the things of this life, with which He has blessed us, as opportunities to bless others. In this way hearts will be fixed on Him and not on the elusive satisfaction of the treasures of this life. This is what Paul encourages the believers who live in Colossae to practice as their way of life. 'If then you have been raised with Christ [to a new life, thus sharing His resurrection from the dead], aim at and seek the [rich, eternal treasures] that are above, where Christ is, seated at the right hand of God. And set your minds and keep them set on what is above (the higher things), not on the things that are on the earth' (Colossians 3:1–2, AMPC).

Jesus has just been encouraging the people to seek God's kingdom above all. To let go and hold everything of this life loosely. He declares that their heavenly Father knows everything they need, and is giving the kingdom to them. What greater incentive could there be? Trade the trash of this life for the treasures of heaven. Trade failure and disappointment for His life and satisfaction. Trade a pale shadow for the pure substance. It sounds like a no-brainer. If the pure substance and kingdom treasure seem more elusive than the shadow and trash, then we need to strengthen our resolve to pursue Him even more strongly and passionately. Maybe He is not 'big enough', which speaks of a lack of faith in who He really is, in His word and promises. Maybe the disappointments and unanswered prayers and the constant struggles have caused faith to seep out and leave an empty space where faith used to be strong. Perhaps there is a misconception about Holy Spirit, which has relegated Him to a false reflection of His true Being. Whatever may be the case, God is good, all of the time, in every situation and circumstance. It is His character and nature. He cannot change. He is the same today as yesterday and will be for ever. He is Truth and true, for the same reason. He is always faithful, for the same reason. Whatever our circumstances may scream at us, God is to be trusted because He is God. He is perfect, true, and good in every way, always.

I wonder who, what or where is your treasure today? Does it give you pleasure beyond the immediate?

I read recently an insight into Jesus' prayer life. It had me thinking. I was deeply affected by this thought and saw the invitation from Father God to reach into Him for such a heart. We read regularly in the Gospels that at the end of the day, Jesus would go somewhere apart to pray. His days were very busy and tiring. Life-giving teaching, compassion-filled miracles, challenging confrontations, miles walked surrounded and buffeted by excited, noisy crowds, such was a typical day for Jesus. Then He goes off to pray. Not for Him the mind which thinks, 'I've earned a rest. Take the phone off the hook, put your feet up, enjoy a good movie on TV, spoil yourself with chocolate, wine, coffee, or whatever. Just let me unwind, I need to relax!' No, Jesus hurried to the place He most desired to be. Time alone with the Father. Prayer was Jesus' reward for all His faithful obedience. Wow! You see, Jesus viewed prayer not as a duty, or chore, not as something to be tagged on to being a Christian. For Him it is the sheer joy of being totally enraptured by the Father's Presence. He can fully concentrate on loving and enjoying this time, without distractions. No questions, no complaints. Simply at One in every way with His Father. Loving and being loved, blessed, encouraged and refreshed. His heart at 'home'.

Jesus is living out the truth of His words 'where your treasure is, there will your heart be also'. Allow me to take a look at the treasure of Jesus' heart.

'The Son can do nothing by himself; he can only do what he sees the Father doing, because whatever the Father does the Son also does. For the Father loves the Son and shows him all he does' (John 5:19-20); 'I seek not to please myself but him who sent me' (John 5:30). Notice how close Jesus lived in the Father. Close enough to see what was happening in heaven. Humble enough to know that without the Father's revelation and overflow of Holy Spirit, He was impotent. He had a heart with only one desire, to please the Father. As He testified in prayer, 'I have brought you glory on earth by completing the work you gave me to do' (John 17:4, NIV 1984). The writer of the book of Hebrews emphasises this when, speaking of Jesus, he quotes Psalm 40:6-8. Depending on which version you read, you find phrases such as:

> 'I have come to do your will, O God'
> 'I desire to do your will, my God' (NIV)
> 'I delight to do Your will, O my God' (e.g. NKJV, AMPC)

The obvious emphasis of these words is that Jesus' delight and purpose was singular. To always completely please the Father by totally fulfilling everything the Father desired. The Father's will is the Father's pleasure. Here is His treasure. How powerfully victorious Jesus' declaration from the cross, 'It is finished' (John 19:30). 'I've done it! Everything! Just as the Father wanted.' Hebrews 12:2 speaks of Jesus enduring the cross for the joy set before Him. His joy is not only in His reward, you and me as His promised Bride, but also that great satisfying joy of presenting to His Father the complete accomplishment of what He embraced in His love for the Father. Where your treasure is, there your heart will also be.

With Jesus as our example, it inspires me into the discovery of the wonders of the Father, as He knew them to be. If Jesus could follow the path to and through Calvary in His love for the Father, then *Abba* God must be so much more than any of us conceive. I see nothing in Jesus' relationship with the Father that suggests He was ever scared of the results of getting it wrong or letting God down. I suspect you are thinking along the lines that it was different for Jesus because He is God and was God back then. And I am just 'me'. The Bible tells us that Jesus, 'humbled himself' to become a man. It also says 'he made himself nothing', becoming a human servant (Philippians 2:6–11). I understand these words to tell us that Jesus, as a man, chose not to use His 'God-ness', but as a man, to function exclusively out of the fullness of the Holy

Spirit within Him. He knew the thoughts of men, not because He was God, but because He was submissive to the Holy Spirit within Him. He healed the sick, not because He was God but because He yielded Himself to the overflowing power of Holy Spirit within Him. This is what gives legitimacy to His words that we will do what He did, and more than that. If such things could only be done because He was God on earth in human form, it puts such promises beyond anything we can experience. In the same way, as men and women, we can only live for God out of the Holy Spirit within us. He said that He could do nothing by Himself, just as we cannot. Jesus, the Anointed One, enjoyed an amazing relationship with the same heavenly Father we confess. The same power that raised Him from the dead works in us also (Ephesians 1:19-20). Jesus left us an example in all things that we may follow in His steps (1 Peter 2:21; Ephesians 2:10). I want my heart and will to be set on knowing Father God to the point of such devoted love. That I love not my life unto death, and delight in doing His will, or pleasure. So that the treasure of my heart will be God alone, unchallenged.

Another aspect of treasure is that of a treasure house. According to my dictionary, such is a place, or collection, in which many valuable things are located. The psalmist tells us that in God's Presence there is fullness of joy, and at His right hand, which symbolises power and strength, eternal pleasures (Psalm 16:11). His promises are not written to taunt us, or knock us down. They exist to fill us with hope and faith and to excite our passion to pursue Him until we actually experience these eternal realities. Eternity is not only waiting for us when we depart this earth, we are living it now, in Jesus. We have passed from death to life, never to die again.

We know from the Scriptures that Jesus is the Truth; our

Treasure, Price and Value

Peace; the Faithful One; a Friend closer than a brother; the One who cares more than any human mother; the Giver of Joy; the only One who truly and fully satisfies the deepest longings of the heart; the Giver of Grace to answer whatever our need may be. He is the One who has more to reveal to us than we have yet realised. I include here a post from my dear friend Richard Barker, whose blog 'Richard's Watch' is always an eagerly awaited message from the Holy Spirit that so spurs me on to higher things in Father.

It is from the end of December 2014 and is from the teaching of C. Baxter Kruger.

And His Name shall be called Immanuel. God is with us! The incarnation is the single most beautiful and inviting thing to have ever happened in all of history. That the God who we kept distant, broke through our preconceived notions and obliterated our false views of Himself. We denied Him access to ourselves yet came inviting us to Himself. He came wrapped in humanity as a faithful High Priest. In order to present us spotless, blameless and without reproach. He wrapped Himself in what was our fall in order to raise us up together where we first came from. In Him was LIFE and that LIFE was the LIGHT of men. He came running like a Father of long lost sons. Running to embrace everything un-embraceable. He came to restore back the DNA of our Father. He included us in His relationship with Father and Holy Spirit. He welcomed us inside the beauty of the Trinity. He made us one with Him just like He is One with the Father.

He prepares a table of delicacies for us. He cooks for us. He serves us. He washes our feet. His anger rises against our enemies. They scatter. He plows our soil for His seed. He waters it. He gives the increase. He joins Humanity with

Divinity for Eternity. Never to be separated again. He came to set the record straight about Who He really is. He came to ransom us out of the enemy's hand...and accomplished it. He came with God's blood in order to pour it out on our behalf.

He came and invited us to His *perichoresis*. He became like us so we could become like Him. He came to never leave our side. He came and submitted Himself to us. God became flesh and walked with us. He travelled our roads and experienced our experiences. He hugged us. He kissed us. God loved us when we hated Him. He allowed our rejection of Him only to find Him on the other end waiting. God is with us through the thick and thin. Never to leave or forsake. Forever entwined. His Glory, a cocoon of Himself in process of transfiguring us, metamorphosis. He came to that which was birthed out of Him. His own creation spitting at Him and reviling He who made them. Yet He embraced them by submitting to their way of death. He laid His life down by our hands. He exposed the principalities and powers making an open show of them. We cursed, He blessed. We lunged at Him, He didn't move.

We accused, He didn't defend. God with us. God in us. God for us. God exists. God is here for you to experience in all His fullness. He came to rend a veil. Not only for our access of Him but His access to us. He came to reconcile. He came to forgive. He came to set the prisoners free. He came to destroy religion. He came to reveal our Father. (The Great Dance. The Christian Vision Revisited.)

Truly He is a 'treasure house' of spiritual life and goodness. Oh, the joy and excitement of unimpeded access to this house of abundant treasures! To be free to search out and claim the riches of His unfathomable grace and never-ending love. 'Come

Treasure, Price and Value

to me', said Jesus: 'If you are thirsty, come to me and drink!' (John 7:37, CEV). Such a big word, 'if'. Everything depends on the magnitude of that 'if' in the life of each of us. It takes time to get to know someone in this way, and we all have time. No matter how busy our day, we all have time. Driving the car? Time to worship and pray. Preparing a meal? Time to worship and pray. Relaxing in the garden? Time to worship and pray. It revolves around 'if'. Jesus is always with us, always in us; He promised that whatever we are doing, He is there. Sharing our busyness with Him brings Him into our consciousness in a greater way. I repeat, we all find the time to do the things we want to do. If we do not have time, we are too busy and need to reassess our priorities. I say this having brought up six children, one of whom has needed 24/7 care from birth. We give our time and energies to those things which give us pleasure. How can we exclude Jesus from this scenario?

I remember my children, during their childhood, excitedly searching out the 'treasures' under the Christmas tree. Total focus, grabbing everything that had their name on it. Tearing off the wrappings, ripping open the packaging to claim as their own what had been so lovingly thought about and set apart. There was no letting up. No being content with one gift while several others remained unopened. Everything had to be claimed, and owned till there was nothing left.

In the story of the youth who demanded his inheritance, then squandered it in thoughtless, self-centred behaviour before coming to his senses and returning home to a royal welcome, there are some very significant lessons to be grasped. To begin with, he is welcomed with delight and complete restoration. His confession of wrong causes the wiping clean of his history. It occasions great feasting, singing and dancing. His father emphasises that he is fully restored to honour and sonship. Then comes the sad side of the story. The angry, vengeful older brother who refuses to forgive and extend love and friendship. He wants his idea of justice before any possibility of reconciliation. This son has faithfully continued to work for his father and is aggrieved at this lavish, heartfelt, joyful blessing of the younger son. He displays the heart of a religious man who has spent his years ignorant of the wonderful relationship he could have enjoyed with his father. He has missed out on the greater thing. 'All these years I've been slaving for you and never disobeyed your orders' (Luke 15:29). He has seen himself as a slave, not as a son. He saw his place of privilege as being a slave, an outsider, owned, totally disenfranchised, no true home, no family relationship. He speaks of his brother as 'this son of yours' (Luke 15:30). He is incapable of recognising true relationship. How many believers are so focused on their service for God that they miss the most important thing? The 'one thing … needful', which Mary embraced (Luke 10:42, KJV)? How many are exhausted? Caught up in a conveyer belt Christianity of churning out 'doing for God', while taking their eyes off the One they are serving? Missing out on the treasure of being a son? (We are all sons of God according to Scripture, since it was always sons who inherited.) This son missed out on so much. Seeing himself as a slave, he complains that the father never gave him anything. Did his slave mentality keep him from enjoying what was his by right of birth? I believe so, since the parable tells us that.

He had a complaint against the father. Do you have complaints against Father God?

'All these years, and what do I get out of it?'

'Why God?'

'All these prayers and no answers.' And so on.

Treasure, Price and Value

The father answers with 'My son' – he is no slave, not in truth. He is a son, the heir. He is the one seen by the father as his beloved, his son, valued, loved. One to be delighted in. The father sees relationship. The son sees service. But here we have the father affirming his son. He is not a slave. Father is speaking relationally, 'you are always with me'. Then he makes this outrageous statement, 'everything I have is yours' (Luke 15:31–32). Everything! Imagine sitting on a fortune without realising it. Imagine living as a pauper whilst having incalculable wealth. This is the position this son was occupying. The inference from the text means, 'You don't need to ask, help yourself, it is all yours anyway.'

This is the son who comes complaining at what he sees as his father's extravagant, blind devotion to a wayward son. It wasn't fair. Dad should have seen the way he has been despised and laughed at by this worthless selfish creature, called a brother. How many questions and complaints are on our lists to ask God when we 'get to heaven'? What a burden of baggage. Is it possible that when we meet our Father God face-to-face, we will have a list of questions we urgently need to ask Him? I don't believe so. I believe we shall be so overwhelmed by Him, His beauty, grace, holiness, majesty and love that we will fall down in awestruck wonder and breath-taking worship. God is not, never has been, nor will ever be, a benign Santa Claus sprinkling 'Disney dust' over all our problems to make them go away. God gave Jesus as His only answer to every problem. When Jesus shouted 'It is finished', hell caved in, death was emptied of its grasp as the victorious King of kings rose from the grave by the power of the Father. He declared His sacrifice acceptable, sufficient, the answer to sin in whatever form it presents itself. Now, by faith, the believer has access to 'everything I have is yours'. We are joint heirs with Jesus (Romans 8:17; Galatians 4:1–7).

Discovering the amazing outcomes of the death and resurrection of Jesus is key to unlocking the 'treasure house' into the realities of new covenant life. The huge gulf between what we read in the Bible and what we generally experience will decrease as, by faith, we take hold of the truths of being a son in relationship with Father God. Salvation is not exclusively about dealing with sin. It is about bringing us into right relationship with the Father – 'no one comes to the Father, but by me' (John 14:6, RSV). Jesus' purpose was always to bring us back to the Father. It was also about recreating us to become just like Himself, so that we fit comfortably and properly in His Presence.

Could there ever be a 'treasure house' to compare with this? We are made complete in Christ Jesus. Where is your treasure, today? Where is your pleasure today?

Jesus' eternal Treasure is the Father. That is where is heart is fixed. I believe the Scriptures illustrate for us the depth of relationship between the Father and the Son. At His baptism Jesus receives the affirmation, 'You are my Son, whom I love; with you I am well pleased, or, 'in whom I take pleasure' (Luke 3:22). The Father has had no opportunity to take pleasure in Jesus' service, as His ministry has not yet begun. The Father's pleasure is found simply in Jesus being His Son. Later on, at the Transfiguration, Jesus receives the same affirmation. He is loved and valued equally because He is a Son as He is for the faithfulness of His obedience to the will, or pleasure, of the Father. Jesus confirms this in His own words, when He states that the Father has set His seal of approval on Him (John 6:27). He speaks of the Father glorifying Him (John 17:1–5). Jesus testifies of the Father's love for Him as He lays down His life for the sheep (John 10:14–18). He speaks of the Holy Spirit being sent in His name as well as that of the Father (John 14:26).

I know my heart reaches out to those who affirm me and who speak of pleasure in me. Do you remember, as a child, receiving praise from a parent who has watched as you fulfil a responsibility they gave you? Do you remember being told how loved you were simply because you were their child? So Jesus lives in this place of constant affirmation and delight. We love Him because He has first loved us. Jesus enjoyed the Father's love with every breath He breathed. We are recipients of the Father's love with every breath we breathe, even when we are not conscious of it. If we can but grasp this glorious truth, how much more would we love God? In Jesus' prayer recorded in John 17, Jesus declares that we are loved in the same way He is. Our Father God loves us just as He loves Jesus. How am I able to be so lukewarm with such glorious truth surrounding me every moment?

Do you know this experience? Aren't there times when we become distracted, even indifferent to God's love? I believe the answer is to quickly confess and repent, in faith receive the forgiveness and cleansing we are promised, and choose to enjoy the fullness of that restored reality of relationship. Allowing His incredible love to permeate every fibre of your being, your thoughts, feelings, attitudes and emotions to the point where you are 'pickled' with love. This is where the abundant richness of His love becomes the powerhouse of all we are and do.

It is so important to believe what Father God says about us, not what our own mind and experience tell us. God cannot lie. Therefore when He states that you are righteous, then you are righteous. When He says you are His beloved, then you are His beloved. When He speaks of loving you with an everlasting love, then you are loved, without pause or condition, without any self-effort to 'be perfect'. The book of Romans in chapter 8 declares that we are already glorified in Jesus. God, who always sees the end from the beginning and who lives in the permanent 'now' sees you as fully justified, fully glorified in Jesus. The more I choose to believe what God says, to agree with His account of things, the more I am likely to grow into the reality of it on earth. And the freer from self-condemnation and failure I can become.

It is God who is working in us what gives Him pleasure. His delight is that we become completely like Jesus, being drawn into that great, eternal, love-life dance of the Father, Son and Holy Spirit. The cross speaks loudly of how valuable and precious you are to God. It demonstrates the length, depth, height and breadth of what God would go through to win our hearts. 'Because you are worth it' could be His accolade. In the ages of eternity past, long before creation was spoken into being, you were in God's heart. He has known you and loved you from eternity to eternity. I cannot repeat this too often. It is such an incomprehensible glorious truth. God desires that I be joined to Him in Jesus. To be one with Him. It makes Him happy, gives Him pleasure. Never allow self-doubt, rejection, condemnation, insecurity, shame or fear to rob you of this life-affirming wonder. 'You are My beloved son, you are My beloved daughter. I am so pleased with you.'

When you look at the human lineage of Jesus, you find incest, murder, adultery, prostitution. This is the bloodline of Jesus the man. He chose to embrace this way to include and draw to Himself everyone, without shame or discomfort. The Holy God of all eternity tore open the heavens, wrapped Himself in humanity, made Himself helpless, dependant. He was born among the straw-strewn mess of an animal shelter. He got His hands dirty to make clean and free the hearts of failed, distorted,

Treasure, Price and Value

fearful, lost humanity. And it was with joy that He did it. The joy of us being fully restored, at one in Him. All because you are treasure in His heart.

- Is Jesus treasure in your heart?
- Is He the treasure of your heart? For, where your treasure is, there your heart will be also.

Chapter 9
Ecclesiastes

The book of Ecclesiastes was written by a man towards the end of his life. A man who was king of all Israel. A king whose wealth and power enabled him to experience anything and everything he desired. For this reason it seems reasonable to take note of his observations and experiences. Both of which came about in the context of a man who has seen the acts of God from childhood at the side of his father, King David, the king known as the 'man after [God's] own heart' (1 Samuel 13:14). Solomon is the king who saw the glory of God fill the newly built temple in Jerusalem. So great was this glory that no one could stand, no one could function. He was also a man of faith, as is revealed in the story of his life across the pages of the Scriptures. A man of prayer and humility. A man of faithfulness and of disobedience. A man whose testimony demands to be listened to and pondered upon. Thus he pens these words. His life has been spent seeking delight and pleasure. All those things that challenge our focus and are used to tempt us away from Jesus, are part of Solomon's story. This is why I am exploring his experiences and understanding. I want it to help us see the comparisons between the things of this life and the things of the Spirit.

I find it interesting that he begins with the declaration that everything is meaningless, or empty. The man who had all power and wealth, reputation and honour, declares that what he has experienced is meaningless. Life goes round and returns to its

The Pursuit of Pleasure

inevitable cycle and our moments of being are incidental to this. I find it somewhat ironic that I am writing this at the turn of the year. A new year is about to dawn. Ironic because I cannot understand the celebrations surrounding New Year. Don't misunderstand me, I love a party. I never need a specific reason to enjoy a party. My Father God sets a table in the wilderness. He prepares a table right in the face of my enemies. He has a wedding banquet prepared for those who are the Bride for His Son. My first book, *Feasting on the Father* is centred on a party wrapped in His love. But, celebrating a change in the date? What makes that worthy of celebration? The date changes every day! The problems of the world are the same. The fears in your heart are the same. The loneliness, emptiness, sickness, tax bill are all the same. So, what is being celebrated? What justifies the spending of millions of pounds on fireworks and attendant needs, in my nation's capital city? Money that could have meaningfully eased the poverty situation for many. Or the homeless situation for many. Or the urgent surgery for many. But, no, some sort of blindness forces people to go through this cultural ritual. What is happening is that nations press the superstition button. A fierce desire that the coming year will provide all the things everyone is hoping for. No more bad stuff, sunshine all the way! Forgive my naivety, but changing the date will have no effect in any way on what happens in your life. I have been through over seventy new years of national celebrations. I can add my own voice to the futility of date-change superstition. This is the meaninglessness that Ecclesiastes speaks about.

The Teacher here is pointing out that the daily routine of rising early; going to the workplace; earning his bread; returning home to loved ones or to an empty dwelling; studying; storing; planning; dreaming, all is empty and meaningless. The global

Ecclesiastes

economic collapse shows us how fragile and insecure even the largest of global corporations can find themselves. How many people are chasing that elusive dream of happiness depicted as a comfortable lifestyle without financial worries? The dream of happy, well-adjusted children and faithful relationships? It sounds so good, so right, and so desirable. Then, along comes sickness, or redundancy, and everything changes. The security surrounding our dream crumbles and we flounder in fear and uncertainty. Is it meaningless? A comfortable lifestyle, secure relationships and well-adjusted children are good things for us to enjoy, I am not suggesting otherwise. But there is so often a fragility attached that reveals how insecure such a confidence can be.

Another view can speak of the merry-go-round on which we are born, we grow up, we work, we earn, pay taxes, marry, produce offspring, grow old, hopefully, then die, leaving everything behind us. Why? Is this meaningless?

It sounds somewhat depressing. That is not my intention, therefore I want to journey through his book with the Teacher, and see if he has any meaningful insights for us within this merry-go-round of life.

He goes off to pursue pleasure. Yes! We are all in agreement with that. Everything we do is to achieve and experience pleasure. How does Solomon do this? He uses his vast wealth and power, so that 'I denied myself nothing my eyes desired. I refused my heart no pleasure' (2:10). He built himself luxurious houses, planted vineyards and drank their wine. He acquired slaves to serve his every whim. He had gold and silver beyond counting. He had musicians to entertain him and a harem to satisfy his every sexual longing and fantasy. Wow! Every lottery gambler's dream come true! His conclusion? 'Everything was meaningless, a chasing after the wind; nothing was gained under the sun'

(2:11). Can you imagine the freedom to indulge yourself to such limitless degrees? I wonder how many of you are thinking right now, 'Yes, bring it on, I wouldn't find it meaningless.' No?

He denied himself nothing his eyes desired. This happened in the Garden of Eden when Eve saw that the fruit was 'good for food' and 'pleasing to the eye' (Genesis 2:9). Then she responded as did Solomon, she took what pleased her eye. The whole of humanity has lived under the curse of that incident ever since. How deep-down satisfying and worthwhile are the pursuits of your life? How would your life look without them? I find it interesting that we in the West live in cultures that are so money and sex-focused, so 'free' to indulge ourselves as we wish, yet so desperately unhappy. Where are the wise and brave ones who will choose to step off the merry-go-round? How many Christians are awake to the truth that the mind-sets of our cultures are generally contrary to God? I wonder how many are realising that this hedonistic pursuit of pleasure is holding them back from the fullness and satisfaction they are seeking.

Solomon was known for his wisdom. He was especially gifted by God with wisdom, since he was wise enough to recognise that the responsibility of leading a nation demanded a wisdom he did not have. So he asked God to give him the wisdom he needed. An example here for all politicians and presidents to follow. Because of his humility and selfless request, God also blessed him with an abundance of the good things of life he had not asked for.

We live in days in which intellect is highly valued. Many universities bestow honorary degrees on people who are famed for their wisdom, and academic achievements. Yet Solomon concluded that 'The wise man has eyes in his head, while the fool walks in the darkness; but I came to realise that the same fate overtakes them both' 2:14, NIV 1984). Now, I am certain Solomon is not despising the intellect. He is renowned throughout history as an exceptionally wise man. The book of Proverbs, containing much of his teaching, speaks through several chapters of the virtues of wisdom. More than once he states 'get wisdom'. I believe what he is saying here is that all the wisdom in the world will not keep anyone from dying. The fool and the wise man will ultimately lie side by side in the graveyard. What is the point of your wisdom if your end is the same as that of a fool?

Science has made the most spectacular strides during my lifetime. Very clever people have changed the face of medicine, of transport, of war, entertainment, social media, education, industry, food, and so much more in the arenas of human experience. We view planets not seen or known to earlier generations. We have pocket-sized computers which can instantly connect us with the other side of the world. So much knowledge at the touch of a button. We can conference connect from our offices with partners thousands of miles away. We preserve food long beyond its natural life. We have also invented greater and more hideous, deadly machines with which to destroy one another. Right now, to our great shame, there are people making decisions on behalf of nations, positively considering what are being called 'designer babies'.

Wisdom would ask questions about morality and consequences. Pride forces itself onward with reckless arrogance. The ability to build a machine that enables many lives to be saved is the same ability that produces a bomb which can obliterate a nation. One the one hand we are wilfully destroying countless innocent, unborn babies, while at the same time, striving to enable couples to conceive. Such a madness of contradictions!

Where is the wise? Where is the one who seeks after truth and goodness?

The Pursuit of Pleasure

The perpetual problem is this, that all the human wisdom in the world can never change the heart of human beings. The despair that pervades so much of the book of Ecclesiastes is summed up in the truth that no one can avoid death.

Therefore, argues Solomon, what is the point? Why even bother working? You spend years working, building some form of legacy or inheritance. There are many who leave behind a tangible testimony to their time on earth. A building, a machine, a business, a piece of art, but who knows how future generations will treat such things? Much is destroyed in the name of progress. So, let us make the most of what pleasure we can devise, for it is all so fleeting.

Also, as we all know, you cannot take it with you when you die. This is a cheerful reality, is it not? But a reality it most certainly is.

Solomon turns his attention to wealth. He questions its worth when, rather than bringing happiness, it brings disappointment and fear. Fear, in our generation, that 'friends' may well love their money more than they love them. Fear that it may be stolen away from us and we are back where we started. Fear that leads to so much wealth, in various forms, being locked away in vaults for safety. Disappointment in that all the dreams still do not satisfy what the heart is most longing for. Solomon sees the rich dying before they can fully enjoy their wealth while the poor live long in the struggle to survive. His verdict on loving money is very much a commentary on our generation. 'Whoever loves money never has enough; whoever loves wealth is never satisfied with their income. This too is meaningless' (5:10). As I mentioned earlier, I remember many years ago reading a comment by the richest man in the world, at the time. He was asked 'How much money is enough'? His reply was, 'Just a little bit more.' There are sportsmen today demanding obscene amounts of money to represent a team. More money each week than five times what I receive in a year.

How true it is that 'the love of money is a root of all kinds of evil' (1 Timothy 6:10). Human trafficking is a horrendous global evil. People valued as no more than cattle for the sake of money. The drug trade with its life-destroying drive to get people dependant on it, indifferent to the destruction, waste and pain of thousands of people every year. To say nothing about prostitution, gambling, immoral bonuses to bankers and CEOs who are well-paid for simply carrying out their obligations of employment. Money means more than life to so many. The Bible has been teaching this for almost 2,000 years, and humankind claims it is outdated!

I am aware that this is not uplifting reading. It is a painful reality, nonetheless. Solomon lived through the experience of all these relentless desires of human experience and longing. He is coming now to more pleasant thinking. He has lived his life. He has indulged his every whim, fantasy and desire in abundance. He has revelled in riches; satiated himself on sex; pursued every passion; received plaudits for his palaces and power; been wondered at for his wisdom – yet concludes that it is all empty. It is all meaningless and futile. He is anticipating the words of Jesus: 'What good is it for a man to gain the whole world, yet forfeit his soul?' (Mark 8:36, NIV 1984) Everything that Solomon has spoken about and all his conclusions are based upon his perspective. On twenty-eight occasions he uses a term not found anywhere else in Scripture. He sees everything as 'under the sun'. His view is completely earth-bound. Being earth-bound it finds its echo in the modern hedonistic view of 'just do it' and 'I'm not hurting anybody'.

Also the deeply cynical and pessimistic view that even good

things aren't really good, and everything is bound to get worse. So why not go the existential way and grab the moment, never mind the consequences. None of us knows what the future will bring. Let us eat, drink and be merry, for tomorrow we die (see Luke 12:19). In all of this, the grasping for the pleasure of the moment is the only thing worth experiencing. 'Under the sun', the natural, earth-based view of all who do not live in relationship with God. Is there a more popular expression of this than in the much-loved song penned by John Lennon, entitled 'Imagine'?

I have personally taken the song to pieces idea by idea and seen God's answer in the Bible to everything he longs for. Imagine. Try to conceive of a world where there is nothing bad. I find that extremely difficult. Every day our senses are assaulted by the destructive actions of people. The futility of hopeless 'imagining'. Only recently it was observed that very soon, the richest 1 per cent will own more than the rest of humanity put together! There is no possibility of humanity by its own efforts or interventions ever creating its idea of utopia. The human heart is steeped in selfishness.

All of this being so, I ask the question, why does so much of the Christian community across the world seem so focused on the fleeting 'candyfloss' enticements of this world's empty fulfilment and satisfaction? God has declared it all to be ultimately meaningless.

Our pursuit of pleasure must be directed to where pleasure resides. 'You have made known to me the path of life; you will fill me with joy in your presence, with eternal pleasures at your right hand' (Psalm 16:11, NIV 1984). Every good thing that the heart of this songwriter was crying out for has its answer in God, and nowhere else. All true believers are carriers of the solution to this global heart cry. The joy and pleasure of these scriptures are

Ecclesiastes

what every living being is desperately longing for. And, when the Teacher eventually lifts his gaze above the earth-bound, he states, 'Remember your Creator' (Ecclesiastes 12:1). With all the stuff of life, remember your Creator.

Solomon has given all his wisdom based on the perspective of 'under the sun'. Rising above the earth-bound into the presence of God brings true understanding. He reminds the young man, who is probably a son, that in grabbing at everything of life with both hands, to remember your Creator. Remember God, to whom we are all answerable. Now his advice is full of true wisdom. 'Do not be quick with your mouth, do not be hasty in your heart to utter anything before God. God is in heaven, and you are on earth, so let your words be few' (Ecclesiastes 5:2). Without God everything is empty, meaningless, a chasing after wind. Tragically the arrogance of the heart believes it has the right to argue with God. To throw rocks at Him and downgrade Him to a god of one's own making. A god who can be ordered about and blamed for consequences. A god who leaves us alone to pursue our own ends. 'Let your words be few.' The psalmist understood this. The revelation has opened the eyes of his heart, and he lets us in to the light, into the truth.

'When I tried to understand all this, it was oppressive to me till I entered the sanctuary of God; then I understood...' (Psalm 73:16–17, NIV 1984). Yes, love is the answer to everything. As this great book reaches its conclusion, we read, 'Now all has been heard; here is the conclusion of the matter: Fear God and keep his commandments, for this is the whole duty of man. For God will bring every deed into judgment, including every hidden thing, whether it is good or evil' (Ecclesiastes 12:13–14, NIV 1984). Enter the sanctuary of God. In His presence is all your heart has ever sought. Everything else is a meaningless chasing

The Pursuit of Pleasure

after the wind without Him. Think about it, when you received Jesus as Lord and Saviour, you realised how much He loves you and how much you needed Him. You gladly embraced this divine exchange. Your sin for His salvation, your old life and everything of it, for His new life in Jesus. I ask myself so many times, why would I want to dig up afresh the old, dead, empty ways that I have traded in for Jesus? Every day new mercy, fresh grace and new wine. I am not suggesting that anyone stop living and spend all their time praying and singing worship songs. Although that does sound like a beautiful life to me. What I am striving to proclaim is that experiencing all the good things of life only has value and true meaning when experienced in Jesus and with Him deliberately at the forefront of my heart and desires. A life where Jesus really is at the centre of everything. Where He is truly the purpose and pursuit of everything we do, while every good and perfect gift with which the Father blesses us, occupies its right and meaningful place. We are encouraged in Scripture to 'set your hearts on things above' and to 'Set your minds on things above, not on earthly things' (Colossians 3:1–2).

I can reflect now on a time when, hurting from disappointment and the pain of 'injustice' from the family of God, I went through a period of confusion. I dropped out of committed life in the Body and drifted somewhat around various fellowships, none of which answered what my heart was desperate to know. I found myself financially secure with some spending money on top. Before long I had a couple of holiday homes abroad. One on the shores of Mediterranean and the other nestling in a pretty ski resort. We had two cars, no mortgage, and a store containing at least 100 bottles of wine. Life was good! Or so I worked at persuading myself. Superficially it was. Winter months in the warmth of the coast and excitement of the downhill slopes coupled with a carefree approach to the 'good life'... But I could not convince my heart. Frequently it would shout at me, 'I'm lonely, I'm in pain, I want to go home.' When it became too much for me, just like the lost son, I came to myself and began to find my way home to the Father.

Now, I had not turned away from God, not really. I had simply relegated Him to the outskirts of my life, because I allowed the externals of man's treatments and my soul's longings for justice and fairness, as I saw it, to pull a veil over my heart and shut it down. I no longer have the holiday homes, or the comfortable finances, nor a cellar full of wine. But, I do have my precious, beloved *Abba* closer than at any time in my life. I would not trade Him for a return to the past, even if it was multiplied many times. Holiday homes are not wrong. But when anything comes between us and our wonderful Lord and Saviour, we have erected an altar to an idol. The outcome is death to our heart and spirit. Our relationship suffers and our heart bleeds. God never stops loving us. It is we who close our hearts to His love's healing joy-filled life and blessings.

Compromise and apathy so easily distract hearts from their true home. The 'little foxes', which Solomon speaks of in his beautiful love poem (Song of Songs 2:15), still need to be caught and stopped from spoiling the vineyard of the heart, so that pure love and joy flow from us to our Beloved Bridegroom, Jesus, and compel us into a life of love to those around us. My friend Fenella Stevenson writes about this extensively in her new book *Catching Foxes: A Book for the Bride* (Bloomington, IN: AuthorHouse UK, 2016). Father God is constantly inviting us into this greater, more meaningful walk with Him. He calls us to live from the life and love of Jesus. He longs for our cooperation, in faith, with His amazing, transforming love, to bring us to the place where love determines everything. The striving to do the right thing and to not do the wrong thing become less as we realise the glory of our inheritance, now. As we live in our true God-given identity, now; as we prove more and more that 'my yoke is easy and my burden is light' (Matthew 11:30) now.

In the next chapters, I want to unpack these last thoughts more fully as we look at our love relationship with God, exploring the Song of Songs.

- Do you think Solomon is correct in his evaluations of life?
- What strategies do you have to help maintain your focus on Jesus?
- Is it possible to be 'too heavenly minded', as the saying goes?

Chapter 10
The Song of Songs

This most beautiful love story offers us a place to explore the wonders of God's love for us and our love to Him. That is why I have chosen to visit it in our pursuit of pleasure. It is a book which nowhere mentions God in the text – one of only two books in the Bible where this happens. The other is the book of Esther. This book is full of sexual imagery and ideas. In this way it is very earth-based. It is about human, physical love. It does not easily (naturally?) demonstrate the spiritual. So, why this book?

First of all, God has made sure this book is included in the canon of scripture, the revelation of Himself in written form. God obviously has important truth to bring to us from the pages of this book. It affirms that sex was God's idea from the beginning. 'Be fruitful and increase in number' are the first recorded words God spoke to Adam and Eve (Genesis 1:28). God is not, and never has been against sex. In the purposes of God, sex is the most intimate expression of true love between a husband and wife. By 'true love' I mean love that gives itself and never demands its own way. Love that gives for the joy, honouring and beautifying of the marriage partner. This is a very pale reflection of the relationship between Jesus and His beloved. His newborn, called and gathered out of the community of humankind, to be His chosen congregation in which He rules and guides in love (Ephesians 5:21–33). What we call the Church. But there is no New Testament Greek word for 'Church'.

Since sex is God's idea and gift, how is it that the Church is perceived as being against it? Sometimes it comes across as something the Church would prefer to not be there, so that we wouldn't have to deal with it. At the same time, Satan puts out the message that he is in favour of sex. That could not be further from the truth. Reflect for a moment how those who are strangers to the love and grace of God in Jesus, the 'not yet Christian' community, amongst whom we live, traditionally relate to sex. It is generally selfish; frequently need-driven; lust-fuelled; demeaning to others; abusive; turning people into objects for personal use and gratification. Across the world, Satan's 'love and joy' of sex leaves the overwhelming number of females, from children to the very old, as victims, not treasures. Used and abused instead of being honoured and delighted in.

For believers caught up in this false expression of love, there is always forgiveness, always cleansing, always restoration and always the right path on which to walk. There is no condemnation, and through repentance the full restoration of the heart in the promises of our Father God.

When we look at the history of what is called the Christian Church, we see so many man-made rules and regulations. The forbidding of priests to marry, for instance, where some even tried to extend this to all Christians. Ironically, many of these religious law-makers were living lives contrary to the impositions they were placing on others. Why is it that even today there are so many who continue to embrace and follow these 'non God-made laws'? Is it because historically, the Church has existed amongst societies where sexual abandon has been the culture and practice? Could it be that the knee-jerk reaction against the beauty of God's gift because of the unrighteous abuses of it, frequently in the name of pagan religions, created a complete withdrawal from the arena, so that we have rejected sex, apart from procreation, as the only answer to what is being displayed before our eyes and hearts? Thus we have this immense historic Christian culture mentality which creates an uncomfortable relationship with sex. Uncomfortable, I believe, because we are all conscious of the pleasurable pressure of sexual desire while the Church at large often suggests it really does not know what to do with it.

In the West our culture is so saturated in sex that it is difficult to separate it from the true and good expressions of sex that God created. As I write, the news media is telling us of the most horrendous abuse of children as historic incidents are brought to light. So called 'safe sex' is being introduced to children too young to handle and understand – far too young to physically engage in, whilst being emotionally incapable of distinguishing the feelings which inevitably accompany such experiences. There is such a cultural pressure for sexual engagement that it crushes and destroys dignity, self-respect and the worth of others. A noticeable outcome is the number of young teenage girls pushing prams, while irresponsible teenage boys and young men move on to pursue their next predatory object of sexual gratification. What a picture it presents of Satan's 'love and joy' of sex. There are so many sexually transmitted infections among us. Evidence of self-centred, careless sexual behaviour. Society has long ago ceased to say 'stop' to such behaviour and, indeed, encourages it instead. Rampant hedonism rules whilst we struggle to deal effectively with the fallout; whilst abortion has become society's answer to unwanted, inconvenient evidence of such selfish indifferent behaviour. In most cases, the innocent unborn are being made to pay the ultimate price to clear up the mess of the night before.

The Pursuit of Pleasure

Many of us, including some readers of this book, I suspect, have been caught up in such a lifestyle at some time in our lives. But, by the grace of God, we can choose to not allow the past to determine our future. We can do this in Jesus, because through repentance and confession we are brought to know and experience the forgiveness, cleansing, restoration and freedom which Jesus provides for us through His blood and resurrection. We have His promise that what He has begun in us, He will bring to completion. What God has done is to perfect Jesus in our new creation being and nature.

The powerfully addictive stranglehold of pornography can be rendered impotent by the power of Jesus' life as we embrace Him by faith. I speak from painful, humiliating experience.

As always, as believers, we need to take hold of the truth that the answer to abuse is not non-use but right use. Then to have the courage, in Jesus, to go on to live in everything in 'right use'. This frees us from a sense of condemnation and shame. It frees us from legalism which says 'thou shalt not', whilst we find that trying to 'thou shalt not' doesn't work very effectively because our efforts are our efforts and not His power in us. It frees us from license in which we convince ourselves that God is OK about it. Well, He loves me doesn't He? His grace is extended to me, isn't it? He knows I'm only human, doesn't He? Well, that last thought is a lie. As you are not only human. You are also alive in the Spirit of God. You are a spiritual being living in a shell of flesh. There is truth in the first two claims. Yes, He does love you. Yes, He does give His grace, constantly, to us. But God's truth is transformational truth. He has loved us from eternity past, perfectly, passionately, purposefully. Transformational love. His grace is gifted to us not to ignore sin, or tolerate, overlook or condone it. God's grace is to empower us to turn from sin and overcome it. This is the glory of the gospel. This is why John speaks of '*If* anyone sins, we have an advocate' (see 1 John 2:1). He does not say 'when anyone sins…' The expectation now is that the Spirit-filled, submitted, obedient child of God will, increasingly, enjoy victory over the temptations of this fallen nature and body.

Now, please stay with me. I am not writing this from some ivory tower of self-achievement. I am writing it from the place of biblical truth and my desperate desire to take hold of this truth and see it become the daily reality of my experience in the power of the Holy Spirit, while facing the same temptations as everyone else.

Within the Christian community, sexual sin probably ranks as high as any other form of sin. It is the cause of so much devastation and destruction. Marriages, families, ministries, fellowships and the 'salt and light' significance of the Church are all casualties. I have had fellow pastors broken and weeping in my front room as they have poured out their hearts over the addictive influences of sexual sin. This is no small thing. It lies hidden by 'Sunday-best behaviour' and our masks of fixed smile and all is well. We need to grow fellowships of such love, honour and respect that these failings can safely be brought to the light and dealt with. We need to talk about sex in our fellowships and grow healthy attitudes, understanding and behaviour. I wish I had had those around me at the time I was caught up in sexual sin.

The Bible tells us that what is in a person's heart comes out of their mouth. So, what is in your heart? 'This temptation is too great for me', 'I never seem to get any victory over this', 'I've been wrestling for years with this and I still lose' , 'It's the cross I have to bear', 'I can't be perfect anyway', 'It's in my nature'. How much of this is faith-based rather than experience-based? None of it, as I read. The Bible calls us to offer ourselves as a living sacrifice and to be renewed in our mind. Paul also speaks of bringing every thought captive to Christ (see 2 Corinthians 10:5). It is a truth that God never dangles promises in front of us that are impossible to take hold of. All His promises have their 'yes' in Jesus. Therefore all the words of the Bible, the God -breathed, life-giving truth, are for our good, that we should experience the freedom Jesus gives us freely to enjoy. The better we know the reality of our life in God, the better equipped we are to embrace His truth and life. It comes back, again, to that close intimate relationship we can cultivate with the Father. Choosing to make the knowledge of the Holy the truth in our hearts and minds. It is worth so much to take time to really get to know our God.

Giving in to our feelings, natural desires and thinking is so contrary to the people we really are in Jesus. Who we actually are in Jesus can be summed up in the words of the writer of Hebrews, who says that through the willing offering of Himself as the One and Only, for all time, for all people, satisfactory sacrifice to the Father, we have been made holy and perfect (see Hebrews 10:14). That tells me that, right now, we are perfect and holy in Jesus in the sight of God. A truth of mind-blowing dimensions and awesome seismic outcomes. It is the truth that God's passionate, unrelenting pursuit of you and me has resulted in this 'greater than the mind of man can truly grasp' reality. Through Jesus and in Jesus we are, right now, the righteousness of God. We are now a perfect fit for fullness of life and fellowship in God. We are restored. He has given us a transfusion of His glory, holiness and power that we become as He is. This is such that to not sin becomes the increasing reality of our life as we stand in faith. Because we are alive in Jesus, we have His life and power to resist the efforts of the enemy and see him flee from us. This is my

The Song of Songs

desire, my prayer that I may grow to be just like Jesus here on the earth. His life in me, my life in Him is far greater than the enticements of temptation. I long to be willing and ready to daily yield all I am to be that living sacrifice in which Jesus lives His life in me and my mind is transformed to see and know from a God perspective, not my own. We are free from the law of sin and death. Free to be the people we really are in God. Living under His grace.

Let us not be afraid of sex. Rather, may we give thanks to our Father for His good gift and embrace it in the truth of who we are in Christ Jesus. From this place I venture into this book of passionate love. This great romance between the king and a young, inconsequential girl. It is beautiful in itself, while representing the deepest intimacy between a husband and wife. More than that, as Brian Simmons expresses in his introduction to *The Passion Translation* of this book:

> Love will always find a language to express itself. Fiery love for Jesus pushes our thoughts out of hiding and puts them into words of adoration. This articulation, out of the deepest places of our hearts moves God and inspires each of us to a greater devotion. Everyone deserves to hear and feel the passion of our Bridegroom for His radiant and soon-to be perfected Bride.

This is the perspective from which I want to reach into the indescribable depths of our God's unfathomable love for us. Then to offer to you the inevitable outcome that such passionate, strong, uncompromising, unmatchable pure love creates in our hearts. A life completely at one and as one in and with Him.

At the very beginning of this Song we discover that the word for 'Shulamite' and the word for 'Solomon' are taken from the same root word. One masculine, the other feminine. The king and the maiden come from the same root. Turn your mind back to the story in the Garden of Eden. See how the man is put into deep sleep, like death, that from his side God may take a part and form woman. She was taken out of Adam. 'Bone of my bones and flesh of my flesh' (Genesis 2:23). Both have come from the same created being. Move on to Calvary, see from the opened side of the body of Jesus, as water and blood pour out, the Father is birthing the Bride for His Son. The Aramaic language of this event opens up a startling wonder. When Jesus cried out, 'It is finished', we rejoice in the truth that He has accomplished all of the purposes of the Father's heart to humankind. Yet His words also reveal, in Aramaic, that Jesus cries out 'My Bride'. His bloody sacrifice is the bride price. He has paid it all to embrace you and me as His most beloved. Jesus is the bride price. See the footnote to John's gospel chapter 19:30 in *The Passion Translation*. Out of His bloody sacrifice has been birthed a new creation community, as He becomes the 'firstborn among many brothers' (Romans 8:29). Hebrews tells us that Jesus is not ashamed to call us brothers/sisters. We carry the divine DNA! Sons and daughters of God in the new birth. Jesus is the Head of the Body, the *ecclesia* (congregation). Therefore we are joined to the Head, therefore His blood runs through our veins. This is the spiritual reality of being in Christ.

I continue to be in awe of the magnitude of the love of *Abba* God for me, for you and for all people. This beautiful love song lifts the veil to reveal the passion of God's heart. It extends a passionate invitation into passionate union with our passionate God. The language and imagery reminds us of our human feelings and emotional longings. Daring to translate it into an expression

The Song of Songs

of God's desire towards us, and our passionate response invites us into the excitement of the heart of our Father through the love in the Spirit we experience in Jesus. David Pawson put it like this:

> An analogy is a fact which is like another fact. For example, He (Jesus) would describe the Kingdom of Heaven in terms that His hearers could grasp. The Song of Songs functions in a similar way. The love between a man and a woman is like the love between God and human beings. Both are real and the former helps to explain the latter. The Song of Songs is saying that our relationship with God can be like that. We should be able to say 'My beloved is mine and I am His,' in the same way that lovers speak of one another. (*Unlocking the Bible*, London: HarperCollins, 2003, pp. 372–373)

I have mentioned words such as 'passion' and 'intimacy'. Words which may feel uncomfortable to some male readers in the light of the object of these emotions, the Lord Jesus. I am, and always have been, a very emotional person. Apparently I tend to 'wear my heart on my sleeve'. So, this language does not affect me in a negative way. I have seen strong men go weak-kneed and tongue-tied in the company of that 'certain lady'. Such is the power of love in us. There is a song which speaks of love changing everything. That when this love is in our heart, then nothing will be the same again. We know it so well in our human experiences and relationships. I am daring to suggest we allow ourselves to respond in the same way to God in the Spirit and not to fear our emotions.

Love is a basic need in everyone. The longing to be loved and to love. God wired us that way. He made us to long for and to receive His love. He made us to want to give love to others. Sadly, so many people live in a prison of pain caused by a lack of love, or an abusive expression of 'love'. Others live in a fortress of fear, having been hurt, humiliated or scorned by false experiences of love. The one has locked themselves away so that the pain is not repeated; the other has withdrawn themselves from experiencing love in case the consequences are no better next time round. From the cradle to the grave, love is the strongest influence on us. Love gives us identity. It tells us that we matter, that we are important. It tells us we have been chosen and are special to someone.

In the first chapter of the Song, the lover speaks beauty into his beloved. She sees herself as weather-worn and dark-skinned, brought on by the sun, as being unattractive. One of the strong cultural evils of our day is the demand to conform to certain ideas of beauty. Billions of pounds are spent every year on beauty and dietary products aimed at producing the 'perfect you'. This is particularly, but not exclusively, focused on the female population. There is tremendous pressure to conform to an expression of beauty that is totally fixated on the external. What you look like. This is not new, of course, it goes back to the earliest days of human relationships. Let us be honest, if guys didn't find girls attractive, and girls weren't swept off their feet by a handsome man, where would the human race be? Would there be a human race? As I always say, when Adam first saw Eve, he exclaimed 'Wow, man!' And she has been called that ever since. God made us different, and I confess, I appreciate the differences.

There are many instances in the Bible in which beauty 'tips' and practices form part of the narrative. Lotions and potions, oils and perfumes play a significant part in the lives of every culture and generation. The most spectacular must be the beauty contest in ancient Persia during the reign of King Xerxes, or

The Song of Songs

Ahasuerus, as he was also known. When the king was looking for a new queen, he sent a decree throughout his kingdom. 'Let a search be made for beautiful young virgins for the king. Let the king appoint commissioners in every province of his realm to bring all these beautiful young women into the harem at the citadel of Susa … let beauty treatments be given to them. Then let the young woman who pleases the king be queen …' (Esther 2:2–4) This kingdom extended from India to the Upper Nile region. There were 127 provinces in all. How many beautiful young virgins were brought to the palace we do not know, but there were obviously far more than your average beauty pageant today. It is believed that something like four years passed from the decree to the time Esther went into the king's presence for the first time. We know that he was attracted to Esther more than any of the other women and she won his favour and approval more than any of the other young virgins. So he set a royal crown on her head and made her queen. The story speaks of the extent to which Esther was prepared for her one night with the king. The one opportunity to impress him. The quantity of oils, perfumes and lotions used on her body must have been enormous. Yes, looking beautiful and handsome has occupied the heart, mind, finances and energies of humanity since we first breathed in the breath of life.

What concerns me most is the consequences of this pressure. Many females end up suffering with anorexia or bulimia in attempting to achieve the perfect body. Untold misery, ruined lives and psychological damage follow this drive for 'beauty'. Add to this the many who suffer such low self-esteem because they do not fit the figure. What is even worse is that little children are now being put into this 'cattle market' mentality whilst they are learning to cope with school. Fortunes are being made as people put themselves under the knife of cosmetic surgery to redesign their shape and looks. This is all in the quest to be noticed; to be wanted; to be famous; to feel accepted; and to feel good about yourself. Into all this the voice of love whispers to the heart, 'How beautiful you are, my darling! Oh, how beautiful!' (1:15) It is the voice of the Shepherd-King. It is the voice of Jesus.

'I want to believe You, Jesus, but it is so hard when I look in the mirror; in the glossy magazines; watch TV; see other people...'

I believe it is hard for those reasons. The pressures on us these days are so strong, so constant, and what we feel inside usually does not help. Do you remember the voice of love calling you to salvation? Remember how you dared to trust Him them? Remember the wonder of coming to know that you are loved by Creator God? That your sin is dealt with for ever, and you are forgiven and reconciled to God in perfect union in Jesus? Are you able to recall how that trust actually became your reality? It is real and true today. It is the same voice that speaks now. 'How beautiful you are, my darling! Oh, how beautiful!' Is the voice of love less true today that when He said 'Come unto Me'? Your identity, your beauty, is not found in your history, nor in your feelings. It is not found in your circumstances. It is not defined by the world around us, nor your experience. Who you really are is found in Jesus. When Jesus says you are beautiful, then you are beautiful. Why believe Him for salvation and not for life? Choose to accept God's declaration about you, then go and look in a mirror. Then say to the person you see there, 'Hello, beautiful.' Man or woman, it makes no difference. In the eyes of God, you are beautiful. This is how He eternally purposed you to be. This is how He sees you today.

This is a major difference between the kingdom of God and the kingdoms of this world. You are incredibly handsome, suave, sophisticated and twenty-five years of age. By forty-five you have a paunch, sagging cheeks and thinning hair. The world says you are past it. God says you are beautiful. It is exactly as the Bible says, that man looks on the outward appearance, but God looks on the heart (1 Samuel 16:7). God makes us beautiful from the inside out. This world is only interested in the outward appearance. As Peter's words say, 'Your beauty should not come from outward adornment, such as braided hair and the wearing of gold jewellery and fine clothes. Instead, it should be that of your inner self, the unfading beauty of a gentle and quiet spirit, which is of great worth in God's sight' (1 Peter 3:3–4, NIV 1984). In context these words are addressed to women, but as I have stated before, I believe the principle is equally true for men.

Now, as a man, I confess to knowing nothing about the inner workings of the mind and emotions of a woman. But I still want to emphasise the point of seeing how God sees us and not sacrificing ourselves to the pressures and false expectations of society. God's beauty is not superficial. It is deep and secure. It is able to withstand anything thrown at it since it is centred in God and the finished work of Jesus. Therefore it is everlasting. As Peter termed it, the 'unfading' beauty. No need for constant lotions and potions to create or maintain the face of the glossy magazines, or try to hold back time. A once-for-all-time operation secured, forever, the unfading beauty which is so valued by God. The disease was dealt its death-blow. The rock-hard heart was smashed to bits. Torn out of the darkness of your soul and replaced with a new heart, a heart of flesh filled with, and by, love. The only heart that could fit, live and function within a new creation being.

The recognition of who she is in the eyes of her beloved emboldened the girl to engage in a dialogue. Taking to heart his words of endorsement, affirmation and passion, she is filled with confidence to express her heart to the king. Do you remember, as I do, when as a love-sick youth, stumblingly telling the object of your desire that she was pretty (or, for girls, he was good-looking)? In the joy of hearing those words, she shyly smiled, then ventured to tell me that I was quite handsome also. Well, here the maiden finds herself in that position. Receiving words of love and growing into them, she offers to the king what is in her heart. 'How handsome you are, my lover! Oh, how charming!' (1:16, NIV 1984). For many Christians, God remains at a distance, an austere despot. One who is more concerned with our failings than the glories of our adoption. Life is about doing things for God more than being His chosen, beloved child.

The depth of His love for us is seen in the fathomless gift of Jesus as our Saviour bringing us, by faith, into this loving relationship with the Father. Making us one with Him. The Westminster Catechism states that the chief end of man is to glorify God and enjoy Him forever. Enjoy Him, forever. God's kingdom is a kingdom of joy. Can there be joy where there is fear? Can there be joy where the fear of judgement or failure exists? Such a view of God is so contrary to the representation of Him throughout the Scriptures, seen most perfectly in Jesus. Jesus said, 'Anyone who has seen me has seen the Father' (John 14:9). Jesus is a man of pure love. His willing sacrifice demonstrates the heart of God. God so loved that He gave. He gave from His relentless pursuit of us to have us back where we belong, in Him. This is the God who constantly calls to our hearts.

Our God is so beyond our comprehension, but we see glimpses of Him as we read the Bible. We have the words of hymns and songs which, as well as aiding us in worship, give us pictures of His awesome majesty; His breath-taking beauty; His love and goodness, and so much more. This is the One to whom you can say, 'How handsome you are, my lover! Oh, how charming!', using whichever words most easily speak what is in your heart. How He loves those times when we whisper our devotion and feel His embrace. Times when we know that we love Him and are free to tell Him. How do I know this? Because He is our Father. Every father loves to give and receive love. Even those human fathers who, in their pain and fear, have failed to demonstrate love. Deep in their being they continue to long for love and to know the ability to share it. Our God is the Perfect Father, in every way.

The bride-to-be expresses why she is so captivated and overwhelmed by her lover. She declares, 'My lover is to me a sachet of myrrh between my breasts' (1:13, NIV 1984). It is easy to skip over these words without catching the significance of them. Myrrh is a symbol of suffering. It speaks to us of the cross of Jesus. It was a common embalming spice. It is this poignant image that reveals the core of devotion and love that strikes right at the deepest place of need and longing. It pierces to the depth of every desire and ambition. It reveals the nakedness of our soul without the clothing of grace and righteousness. The sachet of myrrh is sitting as close to the heart as is possible. It is Jesus, in His dying, who slays us to bring us to life. So enormous is the price He paid, freely giving Himself. Taking to himself every wrong thought, word, desire, action and attitude we have ever had. Then to embrace them in His pure heart and carry them to death, where they lay dead forever; more than that, where they have been obliterated, no longer existing. The grave in which they were buried lies empty. He has erased them from our hearts, erased them from our history, and He cannot find a record in heaven that they ever existed. So effective is the offering of His blood on the altar of His body. So powerful is the victory of His resurrection life. 'This is how precious you are to Me,' is what His crucifixion declares. It shouts a resounding 'no' across the aeons of eternity: 'Sin will not prevail. It will not spoil My glorious intention for you. For you in Me and I in you, in the eternal dance of perfect Oneness.' When this glorious good news bursts into our consciousness, into our souls, what else can we do but love, worship and gladly yield the ownership of our whole being to Him? This is the place where believers make their choice, the place where myrrh sits close to our hearts. Jesus gave His all for you, how will you respond to that? This is the most important question every person will ever have to answer.

I know I am unable to grasp the magnitude of that event and all it signified and achieved. But I do know that for me, the truth that God knew me before creation came into being, that I am so significant to Him that He chose me to be His in loving relationship and would not allow the folly of disobedience to prevent that, holds me captivated in love, chained to His heart and lost in awe and wonder. Adam and Eve were put out of the garden, not as a punishment, but to protect them and all humanity from everlasting sinfulness. Having made themselves 'god' by their disobedience, had they eaten the fruit of the Tree of Life they, and we, would be locked, eternally, into lives of slavery to the sinful nature. Their sinful DNA which we have inherited would have been forever controlling and nothing could have changed God's eternal decrees. It was in Eden that God cried out, 'Where are you, Adam?' Adam was lost in the garden, not outside of it. Jesus took that curse of sin upon Himself so that we can return to that 'garden life' that was enjoyed before sin.

Why? Why would Jesus do this for you, for me? My only answer is love. Why would Jesus love you? Love me? Because He is love, and God's love, unlike our human understanding and expressions, is perfect, total and unconditional. Basically God cannot do anything else. He has to love because He cannot stop Himself. Nor does He want to! He is love, everything of Him is love. Therefore the whole of who He is, is delightedly committed to loving you, because He wants to, because He loves you. This is why I am so captivated and overwhelmed by such passionate, committed, relentless love, and why I know I must respond. I must say 'yes'. What else can I do? I know I desperately need and long for this love. Deep in my being is this knowing that this love is what my heart has needed and yearned for from my first breath. It is what God made me for.

On top of that comes the dazzling rest of the story. Not only are we so loved, now we are also completely free from the controlling power of sin over our hearts and minds. We are completely free in Jesus to be the child Father God destined us to be before creation. In Him, part of His family, loved the same as Jesus. We are inheritors, with Jesus, of all that Father bestows on His Son. Fully chosen, uniquely desired and adopted through the Holy Spirit to bear the DNA of God. A new creation being, alive to God in the Spirit. Everything of the 'old' has been crucified in Jesus, erased from our history. This is God's truth to your heart and mind. The truth to penetrate your soul and set it free from the longings of self. No longer a slave to fear, now a child of God. My Father's opinion of me states: 'That's *my* child. He is perfect.' Yes, perfect in His sight. In Jesus you are without blemish, without fault. We all know that our day-to-day experience is so far removed from this, as we struggle with all manner of things that militate against God's truth. We are called to 'live by faith [and] not by sight' (2 Corinthians 12:7). Faith tells me that the Holy Spirit in me is greater than everything thrown against me by the enemy. Faith assures me that because of Jesus I am dead to sin, and sin to me. Faith tells me I do not have to choose to yield to temptation. I am slowly beginning to receive this truth to my mind, my soul and my heart. I seek the reality of the Spirit to prove His power at work in me. For my heart's deepest longing is to become everything I am destined to be in Jesus.

Through faith we can live free from the fear of judgement and condemnation. You are accepted in the beloved. Through faith we can live free from self-imposed standards and pressures. Free from the demands of others which are out of step with Father God's ways. 'You must...' has been replaced with 'Let My love determine...' We do not receive Jesus as a limited Saviour. To receive Jesus is to receive everything He is and has. This is the sachet of myrrh close to your heart. 'Lord, I am Yours. Whatever is in Your heart for me is fine. I know that You love me. I experience Your love, the love that brought me to You. I know that love can never do anything but good towards me. Lord, I want to let go of everything that hinders the free, full flow of Your love in me and through me.'

The discourse continues as the maiden, representing all true believers, the *ecclesia* of God, rejoices in who she is.

Why does the community of believers seem to be imprisoned by negativity? Why do we celebrate being sinners? It appears to be a prevalent theme of many sermons. Weakness, failure, could do better, these seem to occupy many preachers much more than freedom, joy, reconciliation and overcoming. Are we frightened of celebrating what Jesus has really accomplished, or are we still ignorant of that? We seem to lack the courage to openly confess and believe the truth of resurrection life. If you are truly born again of the Spirit of God, then you are not a sinner. You used to be, but Jesus changed all that. No longer a sinner but still subject to the conflicts and influences sin assaults us with. 'I am a rose of

Sharon, a lily of the valleys' (2:1). Interestingly, the word 'Sharon' can be translated as 'His song'. Does our maiden see herself as the one over whom and about whom her lover sings? I am reminded of the words of the prophet Zephaniah, 'The LORD your God is with you, he is mighty to save. He will take great delight in you, he will quiet you with his love, he will rejoice over you with singing' (Zephaniah 3:17, NIV 1984). Your *Abba* God sings over you, sings about you, sings to you. There has to be a reason for this. In the world singing to and of the love of your life is a universal occupation.

How much more when God is involved! What a contrast between the often heard 'woe is me' mentality and the 'bursting with love' song coming from heaven. God delights in who you are, as you are. Today you are the apple of His eye (see Psalm 17:8). I want to increase in being a sponge in the ocean of God's love. Drinking in till I am fully saturated in love. Squeeze me, and I only want love to come out. Can you embrace this? It is the biblical revelation to us of what Calvary means. You have the right to stand tall, unapologetic and unashamed to humbly declare that because of Jesus, you are a radiant, victorious, deeply loved child of God. I know it doesn't feel like it, most of the time. But we are invited to live by faith, not by feelings. Will you dare to believe that God's declaration about who you are is so much greater than your own?

Notice here in verse 2 of chapter 2 that the king, the maiden's lover, states she is a lily, even though surrounded by thorns. Thorns speak of the curse of sin. God told Adam that thorns would accompany his labours as a result of the effects of sin (Genesis 3:17–18). Jesus wore a crown of thorns as He hung, as a curse, on the cross. Surrounded by every expression of sin, feeling the fury of temptation and the shame of failure, our God

The Pursuit of Pleasure

tells us that we are pure in His sight. Lilies represent purity in the Scriptures. They were engraved on the pillars of the temple as a symbol of this. The invitation is always there, to choose to agree with God. He is not going to change His mind, whatever we do. His unchanging truth is secured in the victory of Jesus over sin, death and hell. Your history and experiences do not determine who you truly are. We have freedom in Christ Jesus to boldly confess Him before others, whatever their opinion of us may be. 'He has taken me to his banquet hall, and his banner over me is love' (2:9, NIV 1984). How can we ever be embarrassed or ashamed of Jesus? Look at the cross and hear Him whisper your name: 'I do this for you.' He leads us proudly to His house of wine, which is what the banqueting hall actually is. He has brought us to the one place of absolute sufficiency for every desire. His banquet. A table of never-ending supply of every enticing satisfaction. 'Come to Me if you are thirsty. Come to Me if you are hungry.' What need does your heart have right now?

There is an answer in this banquet place. A sufficiency of grace. An overflow of love, of encouragement. A word of wisdom or revelation. The strength to keep going, or the peace to settle over that gnawing fear. It is all here, in Him, the best Lover and Shepherd of your soul. All embraced, packaged up in His everlasting love. The banner of His delight and faithful covenant commitment.

I confess to being addicted to God. Utterly captivated with Him. I know I cannot live one moment without Him. Nor do I need to, for He has promised to never leave me. In Him we can enjoy the experience of living, moving and having our being. Worshipping Him is like drinking the water of life, being refreshed, revived, revitalised from the effects of the thorns.

Captivated by His beauty, His incomprehensible love, arrested and willingly held awestruck by the wonder of He who has lavished all His love and affection on me, who am I that He should love me so? 'I am faint with love' whispers the maiden (2:5). How lovesick for Jesus are you? For the small number of people in this life whom I love most dearly and deeply, I would walk to the moon, barefoot over broken glass, counting it a privilege, an honour and a joy. Should I confess that for all humanity? Maybe, but I don't believe I am yet in that place. Will I confess this of Jesus? With all of my heart, I dare to say, 'Yes.'

Even though we live in God in a place of rest, we can never stand still. When we stand still, we stagnate. Our unchanging God is always doing a new thing. New wine is poured into new wineskins. There are always fresh places of His heart to be brought into. Fresh areas of our hearts to be yielded to His love. There is no need to fear His call, 'Arise my darling, my beautiful one, come with me' (2:10). There is an old saying that God loves us just the way we are, but He loves us too much to leave us the way we are. And so His love keeps calling, 'Come with Me.' He already knows everything about us and our lives before the invitation comes. There is really no place for 'But God'. He knows already. 'But God' really means I am scared, I don't want to, I like where I am. In His invitation He is asking, 'Do you truly trust Me? Then come away with Me.' You will be glad you did.

Where is He taking us? He is going to show us the little foxes. The little foxes that ruin the vines in the vineyard of our hearts. Remember He loves you too much to leave you as you are. We all have stuff in our lives. Stuff that blocks the strong flood of His love, the joy, peace, patience, goodness, kindness and faithfulness, gentleness and self-control which demonstrate what Father God is like (see Galatians 5:22–23). The fruit of who He is in us. Is it enough to be kinder than I used to be? Or more patient? Is that

The Pursuit of Pleasure

as far as it goes, as good as it gets? We all know that at any time we can 'get off the bus'. We can say, 'I've gone as far as I want to. I don't need all this hassle from God.' He will leave us just where we decide is a good place for us. I find nowhere in the Bible that suggests God forces His love on anyone. But, let me ask a question. Is there anything worth stopping for? What is there that is better than the pursuit of the deepest intimacy with the Father? A more worthwhile pursuit of pleasure? What surpasses being as close to God as possible? Is there a voice sweeter and more full of love than His? Is there a prize of greater value than becoming like Jesus? At one in the Father? Being made fit to be an integral part of the divine dance of incomprehensible love and unity, joy and passion, delight and glory that is the Godhead?

The second chapter of this most lovely of Songs concludes with a beautiful, encouraging image of mutual delight and peace. 'My lover is mine and I am his; he browses among the lilies' (2:16, NIV 1984). The king has already declared his beloved to be as a beautiful lily, and now he comes to browse where she is. How book lovers delight to browse among the shelves of books. Dusty, ancient, new, even, covering every area of interest. Hours spent browsing. Delight-filled hours. Holding great literature in your hands. Carefully, almost reverentially turning the pages. The smell, the discolouration and wear add to the pleasure. Stroking leather-bound volumes and the excitement of discovering a 'must-have' copy. I have some 'must-have' books and I treasure them and feel honoured to own them. Now, picture Jesus, browsing among His beloved ones. Reverentially walking among us as we meet together to worship Him. See how He gently caresses this one and that one with His grace. Stirring up devotion, refreshing gifting, restoring brokenness. So gently, carefully catching up the tears that flow from pain as well as those

The Song of Songs

that flow from overwhelmed, captivated adoration. This picture is nothing fanciful. In the Hebrew language of the Scriptures, the word for 'browse' can also mean to take delight in. Jesus takes such delight in each one of us. We are the joy set before Him for which He endured the cross. Having taken into Himself all the wrong within you and within me, and offered Himself, sinless, a sacrifice to wipe away forever the curse which we knew, could He possibly take His gaze from us for one second? Could it be possible that He would lead us where His love and grace did not sustain us through whatever we encounter? I know, as I am convinced you are, that such a thing is not possible. He is always working for your good in everything that is happening in your life. Dare to trust Him still. Embrace His 'Arise, My darling, My beautiful one, come with Me. Let us catch the foxes, those little foxes that spoil and ruin the vineyard of your heart.' Trust Him that His love is greater than everything that still lies uncovered in your heart and mind. Trust Him. The treasure of His pleasure is waiting.

- Why do you think so many believers find it hard to love themselves as they are?
- Do you think it strange or uncomfortable to view the physical expressions of love in this book as relevant to our relationship with God?
- Why do you think this may be?

Chapter 11
The Song of Songs 2

Continuing the story, most beneficially with your Bible open at this deeply significant book, chapter 3 opens with a lament for the one the maiden has let go away. The maiden, representing the *ecclesia* of God, His called-out, chosen to belong to Him, in passionate grace-filled love, community; the king, showing us Jesus in His pursuit of and delight in His maiden. How easily we cause our hearts and minds to sense the absence of the Presence of God. We have failed Him. We have let Him down in some way. Guilt takes over, we feel ashamed, a failure. 'I've done it again! Surely He isn't going to forgive me this time.' I've driven Him away. How easily these thoughts invade and take hold of our minds. Sleepless nights and restless days. Hope, followed by shame and guilt, then the struggle and confusion. I know I cannot live without Him, yet so easily choose my own way. In desperation I turn back to Him. If you are like me, you have beaten yourself up, and it hurts. I want the hurt to go away. I want to feel better. I want to know the warmth of His nearness once again. *Abba* God assures us that if we will 'confess our sins, he is faithful and just and will forgive us our sins and purify us from all unrighteousness' (1 John 1:9).

And so we come. 'God, I'm sorry, I've done it again.'

I want to let you into a secret here. God doesn't understand that comment! 'What do you mean, again?'

'I've done it again, God.'

His loving smile breaks in. 'I do not keep a record of wrongs (1 Corinthians 13:5). I choose not to remember your sins (Jeremiah 31:34).' God never forgets. Forgetfulness is a failing, a weakness. It belongs to finite beings. God's love is so magnificent that He chooses to not remember our past failures. In fact, He erases them. He wipes them away such that there is no longer any evidence that they ever happened. He cannot remember them since there is nothing there to remember. Away with 'again'. It does not fit our new creation relationship. That scenario is guilt-ridden, fear-filled and covered in shame. It has no place as the experience of sons and daughters of the King of Love.

Firstly, God has promised us that He will never leave or forsake us (see Hebrews 13:5). I cannot find a scripture which says 'except for when I sin'. Father God is not shocked by our sin. It has already been dealt with. Jesus took it to the cross and then to the grave. He rose again, leaving it behind. He became a curse for us, so that the curse of sin could be broken. Every sinful thought, word or act has already been slain, conquered, vanquished, and made impotent through the blood of Jesus. His glorious resurrection brought us into new creation family relationship with the God of holiness. Sin cannot exist in His holy Presence. His holy Presence is where we live. Therefore we have been separated from sin to be separated unto God. We now stand righteous before Him. He who knew no sin (Jesus) became sin for us, 'so that in him [Jesus] we might become the righteousness of God' (2 Corinthians 5:21). This is our legal standing in Christ Jesus. We are clothed, covered from the inside out in God's righteousness. You stand right now as right, as fit, ready in every respect in God. The devil has nothing in us. His accusations fall on deaf ears in the royal throne room of heaven. No jury can find you guilty. Your advocate (Jesus) is your defence. This is who we are in Jesus. Such is His grace. I am not defined by my actions. I am defined by His. So are you.

This is never a licence to sin and please ourselves. This is no mandate for 'if it feels good, just do it'. Why would we truly want to? We ran so gratefully to His open arms and received salvation, forgiveness, freedom from all the grot, fear, shame and emptiness. As a thankful, joyful, laid-down lover, living in love and affirmation, privileged to serve this magnificent God of love, what is there to draw me from His side? Empty promises of something better, I have already experienced, can never satisfy. But, there are times when we all sin. He has wrapped that up in His promised gift, for all time, that repentance and confession bring the consciousness of forgiveness and the reality of being washed clean, again. No stain or mark of sin or guilt to follow us and drag us down. We can look to the victory of Jesus, His poured out life blood, cleansing away forever every spot and stain of sin. It is finished!

So, away with agreeing with the lie that God has left you. His word cannot fail, and it never changes. He is with us, always, in all situations. His heart is always for us. It is not altered by whether we feel it. Do we have a greater cause for praise, rejoicing and adoration? I do not know one. I will say, which is pertinent to what is to come in the next chapter, that we may find ourselves looking for Him in a different church setting. There are times, sadly, when we outgrow the life of the fellowship we are in. In some way, Father God has revealed Himself to us because of the hunger in us. A hunger others do not share. This has been my experience more than once. Our primary allegiance is to our wonderful God and Saviour. We must forsake all others to follow Him. He alone has the words of eternal life. He alone is salvation. Loyalty is good and necessary, but never at the expense of our growth in God. Never at the expense of the 'so much more' which is available in Jesus. This has nothing to do with pride or being too 'spiritual' to associate with others. It is a spirit of humility in knowing that only in Jesus do we live and grow and have life. It is being joined to a life in Jesus. He has set us in the fellowship and life of His Body on earth for our benefit and theirs. The truth is that when you move out of one fellowship, driven by hunger for God, and join yourself to another, you are simply getting closer to different members of the family, the Body of Christ. I am not an advocate of 'church hopping' for the sake of it. But it is right to know the freedom to worship God and be yourself in Spirit and truth. To be at liberty to pursue God with everything you are and have. Why should we not? Why would any believer try to deter such a desire? Jesus is our life. He is our salvation. He is the only resting place for our hearts. He is the One where all the passion of my being finds its true home.

Later on in the Song, in chapter 5, the maiden has another excursion into looking for her beloved. The story recounts how she searches the city for him. She runs into trouble with the watchmen, who cruelly mistreat her. Brian Simmons, in *The Passion Translation*, likens the watchmen to church leaders. Sadly many believers have been cruelly treated by leaders who have failed to understand the passion in their hearts. It has been taken as a personal assault and, in their own insecurity, they have lashed out. It can be seen as a demeaning of the fellowship they have just left. It is so sad that outside of believers' fellowships are many hurting, confused lovers and followers of God who have suffered at the hands of those they honoured and trusted. For all of this, beloved, we must keep our eyes fixed on Jesus, and invite the Holy Spirit to keep our hearts soft and forgiving. Our security is Jesus. It is not the Church, precious as that edifice of the Spirit rightly is. Expressing your love and faithfulness to God does not need to be defensive. The Father's smile is on you. It is in humility we walk and it is in humility that our pursuit of the heart of God will be recognised by those who truly love Him. There is no competition in following God. No competition within the community of lovers He is building. We all serve the same Master. We are all on the same team.

I want to return to the developing relationship that will lead to a wedding. It is in chapter 3 that we see the king in his marriage carriage approaching from the wilderness. A wilderness is not a place to live. It is a place of privation. A place of hardship and dependence. Hosea chapter 2 speaks of how God led His beloved Israel into the wilderness. It was so that He might restore her and lavish His love and favour on her. It is a very beautiful passage full of compassion and grace. In it God speaks of His betrothal, for ever, of His beloved. 'I will betroth you to me for ever; I will betroth you in righteousness and justice, in love and compassion. I will betroth you in faithfulness, and you will acknowledge the LORD' (Hosea 2:19-20). There are times we struggle and complain about some wilderness experience. We feel it is unfair. A loving God shouldn't treat me like that. Read this passage again. See the love that compels the leading. 'Arise, my darling, my beautiful one, and come with me' (2:10). As the carriage draws nearer, the detail and magnificence of it takes her breath away. Does it not constantly dazzle you the way every glimpse of the majesty, glory and power of God overwhelm your senses with how marvellous He is? The king has made this carriage himself. Fitted to his every desire and purpose. It is the carriage in which to transport his beloved to a wedding. A wedding above every wedding ever known to man. The ultimate wedding. As I gaze it looks to me like a cross on a hill bearing the bloody sacrifice of the Lamb of

God. It opens a vista to that wedding day when Jesus claims His Bride. Yet even in this magnificence there is a call to feast your eyes on the king.

This I find very interesting. In the natural world that we inhabit, it is always the bride who is the centre of attention. All eyes are on the bride, including the groom's! Yet here, the bridegroom king holds the focus of attention. No matter how beautiful the bride, she cannot outshine the splendour of the king. Is this why she so willingly becomes his bride? Who else, where else, can she find a love like this? Dear brothers and sisters, where is there, what is there, that can turn your gaze away from Jesus? Who else can captivate your heart and mind more than the One who gave Himself to call you, His beloved, to His side? Just look at the King. And as you gaze on Him, hear His voice singing words of endorsement and affirmation.

> Listen, my dearest darling,
> You are so beautiful – you are beauty itself to me!
> Your eyes glisten with love,
> Like gentle doves behind your veil.
> What devotion I see each time I gaze upon you.
> (4:1, *The Passion Translation*)

Such a satisfying pleasure to our longing heart and mind.

It has always been said that love is blind. I do not believe that. I believe that love sees the beautiful in the beloved, choosing not to focus on the blemishes. Choosing to not allow the faults to predominate and become the expression of what a person is. Jesus has never suffered from this human trait. And, for us, through His death and resurrection we have already been made perfect in Him. Perfect and pure, just as if we had never sinned. This is the truth of who you are in Jesus Christ. The king speaks of the lips of his beloved as 'like a scarlet ribbon' (4:3). Immediately I am reminded of Rahab who hung a scarlet ribbon in the window of her house on the walls of Jericho. This guaranteed mercy towards her and her family, as Joshua stormed the city. It is similar to the blood painted on the doorframe of the homes of the Israelites in Egypt; the mark of their protection and freedom as God's judgement against Pharaoh brought death across the land. Scarlet is the colour of blood and Jesus' blood forever speaks to God of the mercy shown to us in not counting us as guilty in His sight.

In the bigger picture, it matters not one jot how you see yourself. Jesus, the sinless Lamb of God, went through death for us so as to make us as He is. Your opinion of you will never make Him change His mind. The beauty of you is never determined by a mirror, or set of scales. It is settled in His new creation life. Why not embrace His words? His words are life. Too frequently ours speak death. Allow your heavenly Bridegroom to wash you, cleanse you, revive and restore you. Listen to His songs of love. You have a wedding to prepare for. Here is a bride-to-be who is free of any blemish, doubt or fear. No fear of inadequacy. No doubt of His love. No marks of sin or sickness to mar her beauty. She is completely free in His love to be everything that she is. So it is for us.

'... for freedom Christ has set us free' (Galatians 5:1). It does not say, 'for freedom Christ will set us free'. It is a task accomplished.

You will know the truth and in knowing the truth you will be set free (see John 8:32). These words of promise emphasise the truth of freedom. It is an emphatic declaration. You will be free as you embrace God's truth and allow it to shape you and your walk in the Spirit. We are free to love God out of all of our

The Pursuit of Pleasure

heart, and all of our mind and soul and strength. Free to resist the temptations that would soil our wedding garments. Free to receive all the outpourings of His love, which never stop. His words and songs flow like a never-ending flood of ocean depths of His deepest, passionate pursuit of our hearts and affections.

From his own lips the king gives his reasons for this devotion. Read on in chapter 4 as Solomon recounts the beauty of the one his heart so desires. You and me, all of us, as the blood-bought precious new creation race of children of God, those who constitute His Bride, have stolen His heart. The worship and passion of His people so captivates His affections. These words in chapter 4 abound with superlatives expressing the effect that we have on the heart of Jesus through the love we give to Him. Through the beauty in which He sees us.

Weak love is still love, as I mentioned earlier. Little love is still love. The frequent thoughts and feelings that we have nothing worthwhile to give to God other than a few hasty sentences of prayer as we rush off into another pressurised day, with promises of doing better next time, which usually does not happen, is not seen this way in heaven. 'You have stolen my heart with one glance of your eyes (5:9), just one glance. Just one quick whispered, 'I love You, God.' Just one quietly sung song of praise when no one else is around, or simply turning to Him in need, and His heart is captured by you. Such is the fullness of His love, its purity and passion that just one thought towards Him has Him swooning like a lovesick teenager. This, I believe, is what we are meant to see and learn from these words. There is no accusation. No condemnation. No reminder of failed- to-keep promises. No. Here we have a heart that so loves that even the scraps we offer are a feast of delight. How well do you really know this amazing Lover of your soul? Is He truly alive and burning within your heart? Can any of us be so hard-hearted or indifferent as to turn away and not reach out to know the height and depth, length and breadth of this love of Jesus, the most lovely of all? Surely He is the Ultimate Delight, a pleasure to pursue with every breath and ounce of will.

But, as we read into chapter 5, it appears that we may behave in ways which deny what our hearts and minds really know as true. The maiden is in her bedchamber, ready for the night and sleep. Suddenly her beloved comes calling. She is caught in two minds. Her heart is pounding with desire for him, but she feels unprepared to receive him. 'If I get up my feet will get dirty,' is her argument. 'Oh, I don't know what to do. Yes, I'll let him in…' But, too late! By the time she has made up her mind, he has gone. How often we procrastinate and excuse our lack of response to the entreaties of the Spirit.

'Just let me finish watching this movie', 'You can see how busy I am', 'I promised my friend', and so on.

There is legitimacy in every excuse. But, as with the maiden, her lover cannot now be found. His heart knows that something else has supplanted his place in her affections and he has withdrawn himself to help her see the folly of her ways. Now it is through pain and misunderstanding that she looks for him. Could it be that there are times when our tardiness holds back some expression of God's glorious riches of grace and favour? Let's be honest with ourselves, is there really anything in a movie to compare with His Presence? His grace, joy and blessing? Can we be so busy that there is no room for Jesus to be invited to share our responsibilities? The pain of realisation stuns her into activity. I must have my lover. I must know the presence of Jesus.

As she searches through the town she is hindered and badly treated by those who are watchmen. Those, as I hinted earlier, may well represent spiritual leaders. There are times when our desire for Jesus stirs negative feelings in others. They may well feel threatened, or convicted, guilty or ashamed. Turning off the TV causes offence to the careless. Refusing a night out because you've planned to spend time in prayer, or walking away from coarse conversation, such things can generate animosity in others. Is Jesus worth it? Our maiden is determined. She will pursue till she finds. This passion creates an opportunity to tell her story of love. What is it you have? Who is this Jesus you speak so much about? Peter encourages us to always have an answer for those who ask about the hope within us (1 Peter 3:15). This pursuit of Jesus opens doors to tell your story. She grabs the opportunity and pours out her devotion and the wonders of her lover (see 5:10–16). Your story is a wonder, a testament of a great and wonderful Saviour. A story of God the Faithful One. This is the honour of those who will not settle for less than everything.

It reveals the inexhaustible love of Christ Jesus for us. It challenges us, or as I prefer, it invites us to partner with God, as He looks at our ways of thinking about Him and ourselves. He calls to us to take into our hearts His revelation of our worth to Him, as demonstrated at Calvary. He endlessly sings His love songs over us, encouraging and honouring us. His songs entice us to draw nearer. To dare to love and be loved without questions. The only agenda is to woo us into the depths of His heart till we are so consumed by Him that there is nothing to see but Jesus. In so doing Jesus implores:

> Fasten me upon your heart as a seal of fire forevermore.
> This living, consuming flame
> Will seal you as my prisoner of love.
> My passion is stronger

The Song of Songs 2

Than the chains of death and the grave,
All consuming as the very flashes of fire
From the burning heart of God.
Place this fierce, unrelenting fire over your entire being.
Rivers of pain and persecution
Will never extinguish this flame.
Endless floods will be unable
To quench this raging fire that burns within you.
Everything will be consumed.
It will stop at nothing
As you yield everything to this furious fire
Until it won't even seem to you like a sacrifice anymore.
(8:6–7, *The Passion Translation*)

This culminating, magnificent cry from Jesus shows us the urgency of His heart. The urgency to have our all in such a way that nothing again will seem like a sacrifice in the face of His beauty and life-giving grace.

In the next chapter I want to suggest how this devotion may look.

- Do you ever feel 'there must be more than this'?
- Could such intimacy with God be what the 'more' really is?

Chapter 12
Do You Love Me More Than These?

Jesus said 'the kingdom of heaven is like a net that was let down into the lake and caught all kinds of fish' (Matthew 13:47).

I want to share something with you that *Abba* God spoke into my heart about a year ago. He said this, 'You cannot catch fish with broken nets.' It is such an obvious statement, but I have spent these past months praying, thinking and looking to see just what He meant by those words. We read in Matthew 4:21 (KJV) that James and John were 'mending their nets'. The NIV says they were 'preparing their nets'. Every fisherman knows that to catch fish you must have a net that is prepared for the job, and any breaks in it must be repaired. Broken nets will not catch fish!

I ask for your kindness as I attempt to unpack all that this has spoken into me. It comes from a heart that has loved Jesus and His Church for over fifty years. A heart that still cries out 'Your kingdom come. Your will be done On earth as it is in heaven' (Luke 11:2, NKJV). A heart that weeps every time some unpleasant story sullies the glory of God and damages the *ecclesia*. A heart that has been yearning all these years to see the Body of Christ on earth enter into all that Father purposes for us. I have no personal flag to wave save that which I believe God has so firmly sealed in my heart, which is the flag of genuine Bible-based Spirit-filled unity. I take my part in the responsibility of what the Church looks like and how we go about our Father's business. Will you walk with me, then, as I launch into the following pages?

C.T. Studd (1860–1931), that missionary of great renown among the Chinese, is renowned for saying: 'If Jesus Christ is God and died for me, then no sacrifice is too great for me to make for Him.' It is with that in mind that I proceed through this chapter.

Now, I know that the kingdom and the *ecclesia* are not the same thing. The kingdom is the rule and reign of God where His will is explicitly demonstrated. The *ecclesia* is that body of believers in any given locality, as well as any town, nation and across national boundaries who bow the knee and heart to God, the blood-bought born-again community of lovers and followers of Jesus. Of course, the body of believers is the effective community on the earth which demonstrates the kingdom in the way they live and witness. It is this point that I am linking into the reality of kingdom life in the presentation of this chapter. The kingdom is like a net and the fishermen, all believers, are the ones who use the net to catch the fish. God has given us His net of complete unity in the Spirit as an active reality for all who confess His name. We do not have to create unity. We simply have to live it.

All believers in Jesus are called to be fishermen. To catch people for God. I have stood on many a harbour-side and observed the fishermen preparing their nets. God drew my attention to this and told me to focus on the nets. I remember scenes in several countries which have this one thing in common, nets spread out, in readiness for fishing. Fishermen checking them for signs of damage or breakage. I saw this one thing most clearly. Every net has the same characteristic. All the parts of a net are the same shape and size. 'Look! Look!' He said strongly. 'What are you seeing?'

Do You Love Me More Than These?

I was seeing every net with exactly the same characteristic. Nets are made up of 'nothing' tied together with string, or rope. Every piece of 'nothing' is exactly the same size and shape. He revealed the obvious. Then told me to tell His *ecclesia* this most simple yet startling truth. All nets are the same, and broken ones do not catch fish. The only difference we find with nets is that they are made to catch specific fish. The sizes vary according to the quarry. We are fortunate as fishers of men, all people come in one size and shape – sinful and needy. Therefore, every net we use must be 'sinful and needy'-shaped.

There is a deep-seated fear within God's people regarding so-called 'uniformity'. Terms such as 'unity in diversity' are used to legitimise the plethora of denominations and forms of 'doing church'. But a net with different-sized shapes and sections will not catch the harvest of fish that a proper net is made to do. There should be no fear in Jesus building His *ecclesia*, His way. Even if that meant every local fellowship expression of 'church' looking the same. *If* Jesus did that it would be the best possible expression of 'church'. To my heart and understanding, our way is an embarrassment. Unity is so large in the heart of God. Jesus' prayer in John 17 witnesses to this, as does Psalm 133, and so much of the teaching in the New Testament.

I see a move of the Holy Spirit in which the broken net of disunity and different-shaped holes will be dramatically reduced. I see God's desire for genuine oneness in the Spirit being made a visible reality as He illumines the hearts of His people with the glorious splendour of Jesus. This will excite such a passion for Him that will override denominational differences to the point that believers will choose to put down their cherished denominations in favour of true heart-to-heart relationship and unity in the Spirit. Ephesians 4:3 commands us to 'Make every effort to keep the unity of the Spirit through the bond of peace.' Notice, it does not say, 'Make the unity of the Spirit'. That is already a reality for all true lovers and followers of Jesus. Do we love Jesus enough to walk out of our denominational box to discover and embrace the believers who don't go to 'our church'? To do this is to embrace the glory which Jesus has given us. A glory that we may be one, just as He and the Father are One (see John 17:22). This glory is the same glory the Father gave the Son so that the Son may glorify the Father. I cannot see how there can be meaningful glory in the Church until the *ecclesia* in our communities, towns, cities and nation lives in the fullness of the reality of true Holy Spirit unity. To live in unity is to glorify God.

To this the words of Jesus come afresh, 'Do you love me more than these?' (John 21:15). 'Am I such a delight to your heart that finding Me in true Holy Spirit unity is far more important and desirable than the particular part of the *ecclesia* with which you associate yourself?'

There is no fear in the unity of the Spirit. Every expression of Church is to reflect the glory of Jesus. Jesus is unity in Himself, One with the Father and the Spirit. Jesus is returning for a bride, not a harem! To this end the Bride is to make herself ready (see Revelation 19:7–8). To make herself ready, to my understanding, will demand full repentance of all denominationalism. Repentance of her arrogance and self-exalting, as is so often typified in denominations. She will repent of gathering round doctrine and practice instead of the Spirit. She will repent of the walls she has built to keep others outside and to protect precious beliefs. If doctrine divides the Body, it is bad doctrine or else it is rejected in bad spirit. Such glory of God will descend on us that only Jesus will be important to us. Everything else will become peripheral. The different preferences about 'doing church' will be repented of, since embracing what pleases the Father is to override our traditions and familiar ways. '"Do you love me more than these?" Is the pleasure you find in Me greater than the comfort of the familiar?'

This prayer for the glory on the lips of Jesus will become so much more important than our chosen ways of expressing His love in us, and ours to Him. The net will resemble a genuine fishing net. It will not be a man- made, cobbled together, everyone pick your own shape and size to suit you, distortion. Catch fish with that? Some, but not very many. Hardly worth letting down the net in terms of effort, cost and expectation. Yes, everyone who turns in repentance to Jesus sets the angels celebrating in heaven. Every individual is of paramount worth to God. But, let us be honest, we invest so much and receive so little. The fish are getting away. The net is not fit for purpose.

All local communities of believers looking and behaving the same? Why not? Jesus said that He would build His *ecclesia* (see Matthew 16:18). It will look just the way He wants it to look, whether it pleases us or not. I suggest it will look like every believer loving God with all their heart, soul, mind and strength, to the exclusion of all other. It will look like all true believers loving one another as Jesus loves us, and loving our neighbour with the same care and commitment we give to ourselves. Of course, if it doesn't please us, we have some repenting to do. I do not believe what I see today is anything close to what is on the heart of God. We have recreated it for ourselves. True worshippers, the ones the Father is constantly looking for, will worship Him in Spirit and in truth. This is the correct-shaped fishing net. Spirit and truth expressed in love.

The multifarious ways a body behaves is not about so-called 'diversity in unity'. It is about every individual within the Church living in the Spirit as determined by God, for the benefit of the whole Body and in full agreement and cooperation with every other part, for the health and well-being of the whole. It has never been about different ways of 'doing church', or of believing in different things. This is not a popular word. God said it would not be. But it is a necessary word. It is something God has been birthing in my heart for such a time as this. True unity is one Body in one location living in love to show the world what Jesus looks like. God has one church in Bournemouth, one church in Blackpool, one in Crewe and one in Cambridge and so on right across the nation. As a human body functions with every part fulfilling its purpose and every part in complete unity and agreement, so the Body of Christ on earth is supposed to function. But what do we have? We have church 'A' on one street, and round the corner church 'B', and neither knows what the other is doing. That is no genuine expression of unity. I look at the way Nehemiah enthused the returning exiles in their rebuilding of the walls. Everyone building on their own patch. Every patch linking effectively with the patch next to it (see Nehemiah 3). I see, from this image, the whole believing community in our towns working together in the building of the kingdom of God on earth and that building linking perfectly, so there is no weakness, with the whole believing community in the next town, and so on right across the nation. I know I cannot out-dream God. I dare to believe Him that I will see such a day dawn in our nation.

'I have given them the glory that you gave me, that they may be one as we are one: I in them and you in me. May they be brought to complete unity to let the world know that you sent me and have loved them even as you have loved me' (John 17:22–23, NIV 1984). Notice this is a 'now' word. It is not reserved for heaven. It is so that the world may know. It is for here. It is for now. This is what Father God has opened up to me. This is what He desires His children to know so that we may face up to the disunity and apathy that seems to pervade so much of His called-out community.

> Say to My Church that My Son did not die to create disunity. He did not die for fragmentation. He did not lay down His life for a 'pick and mix' shop-window religion to tickle your taste buds and accommodate your personal preferences. He did not go to the cross so that you could build cathedrals and vast storehouses to your pride and prestige. Listen to the words of Jesus!
>
> Words that come from Our Heart: 'That all of them may be one, Father, just as you are in me and I am in you. May they also be in us so that the world may believe that you have sent me. I have given them the glory that you gave me, that they may be one, as we are one: I in them and you in me' [John 17:21 –23, NIV 1984].

'That all of them may be one, Father, just as you are in me, and I am in you.'

'That they may be one, as we are one'.

How are the Father and the Son, 'One'? We know they are of one essence. With Holy Spirit, they are God. It is actually impossible for any division, dissension, isolation or lack of complete wholeness of Oneness to exist in God. Such is the love of each for the other that complete agreement of purpose is always jointly owned and pursued. The Son never comes out with, 'Hey, that was My idea!' or for the Spirit to say, 'I'm not into that, get on without Me'. Such attitudes do not exist within the relationships of God. 1 Corinthians 13:4–8 give us a glimpse of what this love looks like and how it functions. 'Love is patient, love is kind. It does not envy, it does not boast, it is not proud. It is not rude, it is not self-seeking, it is not easily angered, it keeps no record of wrongs. Love does not delight in evil but rejoices with the truth. It always protects, always trusts, always hopes, always perseveres. Love never fails' (NIV 1984). These are words we can understand. They give us a framework, a standard by which to grasp this glimpse, oh so pale, of the vastness and incandescent purity of the glory that is the love of God. This glory has been given to us. Given for a purpose. That we be empowered to be of the same heart, mind, will and expression of love as the Father, Son and Holy Spirit share to their hearts' content. I can find nothing in Scripture to justify denominations and disunity.

Is Jesus loved enough to choose to leave behind the restrictions and isolation that denominations create? Can you dare to believe such a possibility as I am suggesting? Can you imagine the pleasure and sheer delight we would live in with such an expression of Church?

The total Oneness of Being and purpose reflected in the relationship of Jesus with the Father, is what Jesus is praying into being. In John's first letter, he states: 'If our hearts do not condemn us, we have confidence before God and receive from him whatever we ask, because we obey his commands and do what pleases him' (1 John 3:21–22, NIV 1984). Jesus, full of this confidence, is already fully assured of the fulfilment of His prayer, even before the cross. Such is His confidence that He declares that He has already given His disciples, His followers, His glory to enable its fulfilment.

This glory, the Greek word *'doxa'*, carries the meaning of the absolute perfection of the inner excellency of Christ's Being. His full, unsullied Majesty and Splendour. It involves the absolute

Do You Love Me More Than These?

perfection of Deity. And Jesus has already given this to us! We are carriers of the glory of God. Jesus illustrates how this glory is seen as we read His prayer in John chapter 17. He states that He has brought the Father glory on earth by completing the work He has been given to do. Part of this is giving the disciples the words, the teaching of the Father. Words Jesus received and passed on. In faith, the disciples have the certainty that Jesus has come from the Father. These transformed followers bring Jesus glory through embracing His truth and the transformation it brings. Jesus said, 'I am … the truth' (John 14:6). His followers have received Jesus. This is how He can claim to have given them His glory, since He lives within them. This tells me that there is nothing to prevent the fulfilment of Jesus' prayer that we may be one, as God is.

John tells us that 'in this world we are like Jesus' (1 John 4:17). I confess I find the way the NKJV renders these words even more exciting. It reads 'as He is, so are we in this world' – 'as He is'.

Jesus is the One bearing the wounds and scars of your sin, my sin. He is carrying the evidence of every wrong thought, word and action that has been part of our life. The spiteful word, the angry action, the secret deceit, the never disclosed unhealthy dreams and desires, all we have ever or will ever engage in, Jesus bears that in Himself. This is such good news for us! It means we are completely free of it all. He ripped it from our hearts and held it in His. So great is His desire for our perfection. He who knew no sin became sin for us, that we can live in God's righteousness, here and now. We know that He is gloriously exalted in victory at the Father's side. 'That power is like the working of his mighty strength, which he exerted in Christ when he raised him from the dead and seated him at his right hand in the heavenly realms, far above all rule and authority, power and dominion, and every title that can be given, not only in the present age but also in the one to come. And God placed all things under his feet and appointed him to be head over everything for the church, which is his body, the fulness of him who fills everything in every way' (Ephesians 1:19–23, NIV 1984). Not only is Jesus seated in glory, but we know that we are seated with Him in the heavenlies, and we are hidden with Christ, in God. This said, what prevents us from embracing the fullness of the victory of Jesus over all rule and authority and power and dominion? We live by faith, and by faith we are able to take hold of, and walk into, greater and greater reality of what Jesus has secured for us. That must include the true reality of our unity in the Spirit. The 'Oneness' that He prayed for. God showed me what a good, working, made-for-purpose net really looks like. I believe He wants us all to see the same thing.

As I have already stated, the Church and the kingdom are not the same thing. The Church is those people who have been born again and received salvation through faith in Jesus, by the grace of God. And there is no other form of Christian to be found anywhere in the Bible. This is evidenced by the indwelling Holy Spirit. Those who do not have the Spirit of Christ do not belong to Him (see Romans 8:9). The kingdom of God is the rule of God. The government of God in the lives and affairs of those who love and follow Him. The Scriptures also point us to a future fulfilment of the kingdom when ultimately everything will be as God purposes. In the meantime, we can see the kingdom come in our own lives as we submit our hearts, minds and wills to God and walk in obedience to the Spirit. This is the 'now, but not yet' expression of the kingdom in which we catch glimpses of it through the moves of the Spirit in our lives and, through them, in ministry to others. Our life of worship embracing the signs, wonders and miracles which God desires to demonstrate in revealing His love to the needy.

So now, the next part of this jigsaw. We have received Jesus' teaching and taken it to heart. We know beyond doubt that He has come from the Father. All that is required is for us to complete the work the Father has given us to do. These are the words of Jesus' prayer in John chapter 17. What is that work? To love one another as He has loved us (see John 15:12–13). Jesus not only commands love, He also promises its fulfilment in the fruit it produces, fruit that lasts, that remains. This work is not a duty. It is the outworking of love. Ephesians tells us that we are 'God's workmanship, created in Christ Jesus to do good works, which God has prepared in advance for us to do' (Ephesians 2:10, NIV 1984). These 'good works' are not only the necessary good works that all humanity is involved in, as when natural disasters strike, or the ever-present poor, homeless, lonely, hungry ones. This is work that the Father has prepared ahead of us for us to walk into in the Holy Spirit. Work that is exclusively for those who love and follow Him. Thus it is the outworking of the glory of the Christ-life in us. That glory produces the true unity, as seen in God, which was spoken by Jesus in prayer. It should be evident in every locality, nation and internationally, so that the world will believe.

Are you enjoying the pleasure of fulfilling the Father's good works in the opportunities He offers you? It leaves a residue of glory.

All the biblical evidence points to a local geographic community of believers. As I have previously stated there is one community of believers in any locality. The seven letters written to the communities as revealed in Revelation, speak of the Church in one place. Not the churches in one place. Paul's letters are addressed to the believers in Corinth, Ephesus, Thessalonica and so on. These letters are to all the saints in the city. Never to a group of believers within the community. The Bible presents a geographical Church. One Church in the area, or town or village. Obviously with the size of our cities, the believing community is dispersed throughout it. This calls for a group of believers within the different areas of the city, not many groups within the different areas of the city. This is biblical geographic Church.

I can walk for ten minutes within my community and pass a building which houses a group of believers as I make my way to where the group I am committed into gather. I am deliberately walking past family members whom I do not know, and do not bother to get to know, on my way to where 'my church' meets together. The rest of the bad news is that there is no meaningful fellowship between these two groups of believers. There is no reality of unity. There is no evidence of loving one another and laying down our lives for one another. No wonder the 'not yet Christian' community is not interested! I believe this situation is inexcusable. Jesus did not give His life for such a lack of love. He did not lay down His life so that we can cling to cherished practices and beliefs at the expense of loving each other as He loves us. I write this in full knowledge that I am part of the problem, as well as part of the solution.

I am convinced that what God sees as wrong in this, is that we are living and working independently of each other. In so many situations, we do not know the vision and ways of the other fellowship, nor do they know ours. We are ploughing different ways in the same field, and that is confusion. And we know that God is not a God of confusion. The Bible tells us 'this is his command: to believe in the name of his Son, Jesus Christ, and to love one another as he commanded us' (1 John 3:23). Loving

Do You Love Me More Than These?

one another according to God's way, is to love as Jesus loves, unconditionally laying down His life. The Bible also tells us that hating our brother shows that we do not have eternal life in us (see 1 John 3:14–15). If we are not loving one another as Jesus loves, we are living in a disconnection from the fullness of Jesus. Hatred is not only antagonism and a hurtful attitude towards another, it is also a lack of loving. The Bible tells us we have an ongoing debt of love to each other. Does being careless to the well-being of family members resemble love? Does deliberately keeping ourselves separate from one another look like love? How are we able to justify this behaviour while we claim to love God? The desire of God's heart is that we find one another in the Spirit and love one another. Peter tells us 'Above all, love each other deeply' (1 Peter 4:8). Other versions bring perspectives which add 'intense and unfailing love' (AMPC) and 'fervent love' (e.g. NKJV). What grabs my heart the most is the way it is rendered in *The Message* which says 'Most of all, love each other as if your life depended on it.'

It is the desire of God's heart for this reality of love to be seen within our own fellowships. To have and to demonstrate our love for each other with an intense, fervent, life-dependent passion in the love of God. Such love covers over, doesn't even see the many things wrong with each other, as a basis of relationship. Rather, it will love into passionate love each other's hearts for God and one another. Peter wrote these words not to a church, but to all the churches of modern-day Turkey. He mentions Pontus, Galatia, Cappadocia, Asia and Bithynia. There is no one rule for us and one for them. This is written to all the churches, to all believers. We are all called to love and live like this. Excuses are arguments against God. He has already 'given us everything we need for life and godliness' in our knowledge of Him (2 Peter 1:3, NIV 1984).

The tools are in the box, we simply need to take hold of them and use them.

'Passive love', as I am calling it, fails the standard God is looking for. By passive love I mean the attitude which is not hurtful to other believers, not wanting harm to them. A love that is happy for them and the part of the *ecclesia* they are joined to, to go along as it does, while I get on with mine. A non-involved love is, I believe, a contradiction in terms. Love is always active. God so loved that He gave. The burden of God's heart is to see this deliberate, active reality of relationship among all those who confess His Name. What it will look like I do not know. I am convinced that it will look completely different to what we call church today. I believe it has to.

I dream of what it will look like and I dream in confidence, since *Abba* God tells us 'by (in consequence of) the [action of His] power that is at work within us, [He] is able to [carry out His purpose and] do superabundantly, far over and above all that we [dare] ask or think [infinitely beyond our highest prayers, desires, thoughts, hopes, or dreams]' (Ephesians 3:20, AMPC). How it will actually come into reality, I am not sure. As I look at the Christian scene today I see such enormous obstacles erected over centuries. But I choose to speak to these obstacles and declare that God is so much bigger, so much stronger. He cannot be defeated. Every one of His promises and purposes will come to pass. They are found in Jesus. He reigns in absolute victory. Jesus is the answer. Jesus is the means.

This is not an impossible dream. It is not just the lifetime dream of this dreamer. It is the reality of the realm of the glorious kingdom of God. It is the coming fulfilment and, I believe, is now here, in seedling expression of His word that we cannot catch fish with broken nets. The burden of this book is to offer a perspective of God that so captures and overwhelms the hearts and minds of all those lovers and followers of God, that He truly receives the throne in each of our lives. That we become so full of His love and so controlled by that love that nothing else is really important. Nothing else is worth a passing glance. Jesus becomes the absolute, ultimate delight of our hearts such that we count 'everything a loss compared to the surpassing greatness of knowing Christ Jesus my Lord, for whose sake I have lost all things. I consider them rubbish, that I may gain Christ and be found in him' (Philippians 3:7–9, NIV 1984). I long for all believers to join me in this pursuit of the pleasure of God. To strengthen me in my pursuit that we may all see the glory of His pleasure revealed.

God showed me a net. It had various strange and odd shapes. These were shapes representing every denomination, all different while making up the fabric of the net. It was simply an unnatural accumulation of different shapes and sizes joined against each other. It was an aberration. A grotesque, unnatural, man-constructed, unworkable reject. As His tears splashed into my heart, He whispered, with undisguised, inexpressible passion and determination, 'Tell My Church that she has never been, is not, nor will ever be a reject. She is Mine. I gave everything for her, for each one of you, every individual. She is mine, you are Mine, each individual one of you, so special and precious. I refuse to let you go. Tell My precious ones that I am healing you. I am restoring you. This grotesque façade is being removed. You will be seen in all My glory. These are the days for My Bride to make herself ready, adorned in such awesome beauty.'

I believe what I see and am trying to articulate is fine linen, given to take hold of, to own, and clothe ourselves with. So we will be radiant. Put on this garment of righteousness, called unity. Wear it with love and celebration in the knowledge that the world is seeing Jesus. Find one another, know one another, and love one another, as Jesus loves you. Do this for God and also for yourselves, that you may know such pleasures beyond your imaginings.

You see, beloved, the more abandoned we are to Jesus, the more we say 'yes' to God, the more we leave everything in pursuit of Him, the greater the pleasure and joy, the deeper the peace. We also store up greater feasting at that wedding celebration yet to come. So, I am asking, on behalf of our Father God, is there love for Him such that will tear down the walls of denominations to see the loved ones waiting, and needy, for this love on the other side?

The question is really asking, does our denomination mean more to us than God? Is the belief system we have and the way that is outworked through the life of our particular form of 'church' of greater value, significance and importance in our hearts than God is? Our denominations separate us. Every label tells me that I am not part of that particular group.

Every label tells me there are differences between us that keep us apart. I believe that every doctrine and belief that is used to separate God's people from each other is an insult to the heart of God and the sacrifice of Jesus. I will use an example from my own experience.

Many years ago, a young man in our prayer meeting began to speak in tongues. He was very quickly told to stop. Then he was told something I cannot work out to this day. He was told that if he wanted to do that he should go down the road to the Pentecostal church. What I cannot work out is this. If it was 'wrong' in the first church to speak in tongues, why was he encouraged in that 'wrong' to go and do it somewhere else? Good leadership would have explained the 'wrong' and warned of its dangers, not encouraged its continuance among a different group of believers. If this 'wrong' was OK for the Pentecostals, why was it not right among this first group? There is a conundrum which has no basis in God's truth in this. It was either wrong for everyone, or not wrong at all. If not wrong at all, why was it stamped out in this group of believers? If wrong for all, why encourage someone to go and join themselves to a fellowship practising wrong? This highlights so much of our corrupted man-made ways and beliefs. Using beliefs to separate the Body for which Jesus died. To wilfully destroy that for which He gave His all to bring us into One Body in Him. Of which He is the Head. How can Jesus be Head of that which is not of Him (as with the separation brought about because of tongues in the above illustration?). It is the work of the Holy Spirit to lead us into all the truth. Jesus is the Truth. The Holy Spirit leads us deeper and deeper into Jesus. As He leads us deeper and deeper into Jesus so we become truth in increasing measure. In that way our belief system becomes radically changed from what we have always thought was truth and its importance, into the knowledge that Jesus Himself is Truth and everything is to lead to Him and find its life in Him. I am not a part of Jesus because I have great theology. I am in Christ Jesus because His love brought me to abandon everything else and throw my life, with all its sin, onto Him to be received, welcomed, forgiven, and restored as part of that new creation race of which He is Head.

All denominations and streams of Church have a way of 'doing church'. This is most overtly seen in what happens on a Sunday morning. I have been among worshippers who use a set liturgy, and also with those who have a much more informal way of adoring and worshipping God. I grew up in a 'hymn sandwich' format for church meetings, as I mentioned earlier. Hymn, prayer, hymn, Bible reading, hymn, sermon, hymn, go home, with church notices and offerings fitted in. It was all I knew as a child and a young believer. It was the practice I continued when I first became a pastor. This is neither right nor wrong of itself, as with every other structure. What determines its validity and true nature is this: does this structure contain/control the Holy Spirit? Does it give Him the freedom to do what He wants? This question must be applied to every way we 'do church'. Are we making room for the Holy Spirit to exercise His Lordship in and over the events? If we are not making room for Him in this way, then whatever we do is wrong. It is His church, not ours. Jesus said that He would build His church and the gates of hell/Hades would not overcome it (see Matthew 16:18). It is His church. It belongs to Him. He has every right to do exactly what He wants with it. It is not of primary importance whether we sit in silence for several hours, or dance about waving flags and banners. The questions to be faced every time the believers meet together, in twos or threes, or 2 or 300, are: 'Whose service is this?' 'Why are we here?' 'Is this what God wants?' 'Does the Holy Spirit have liberty to please Himself about what happens here?' If the answer to any of these questions is negative, then that thing has to be torn down and destroyed. The Spirit and the flesh are at constant war with each other. Ultimately there can only be one victor.

Worship, the 'everything of my life in devotion to God, for His glory and pleasure', is, in reality, all about God. I believe it has nothing to do with what I want or like. My desire should be to please Him, not myself. If my attendance at gatherings of the believing community are for me, then I am better off staying away. I'm likely to cause a buffer against the Holy Spirit as He is moving upon the community. He gets to me, and 'I' stop His

Do You Love Me More Than These?

work. Worship is all about God. This is why we come together. It is to worship Him. Does it really matter if I do not like these words, or that tune? Do I have the right to object to the format when the Spirit is obviously moving in power and Jesus is being exalted? I am not there to please me. My desire has to be to satisfy the heart of God. Is not this what true worship really is? God is looking for true worship from true worshippers. Those who will worship Him in Spirit and truth. This is what Jesus taught in John chapter 4. God is always looking to find such worshippers. Is it worth Him stopping and looking when He gets to the company of believers you are joined into? Anything less is not true worship.

I recall with a rueful smile the comment that was made every week when the church was being informed of all that was scheduled to take place over the next seven days. The comment went something like this: 'The meetings will be as usual.' Never a truer word was said. Every week every gathering was as predictably 'usual'. This in adoration of the unchanging God, who is always doing a new thing.

A few years ago I was with a group of professing Christians, among whom an unpleasant antagonism existed. The ugliness of religion struck me very powerfully as this group was engaged in a service using a set liturgy from a book. There were people from different denominational persuasions. As I followed the format, with great discomfort, I must add, I was asking God about what was happening in this gathering. It was a very superficial occasion with strong underlying sentiments. God told me that if the books were taken from them, the people would not know what to do. I was so shocked, and saw in such a dramatic way the destructiveness of religion. At the other end of the scale, I have squirmed in embarrassed discomfort as leaders have stirred up fleshly emotions urging people to clap louder, shout more strongly and play their instruments with greater gusto, to really sense the presence of God. Both these examples are anything but true worship, the one thing God is looking for.

Worship comes from the heart. A heart that is captivated in awe of the glory and beauty of God. It is never about a structure, format, liturgy or a clock. How our Father must weep at such tragic, unnecessary ways of seeking His Presence and of offering praise and adoration to Him.

Jesus came to set us free. His death and resurrection is about freedom. Transforming us from sinners into saints. From enemies to brothers. From being orphans into the wonder of sonship. Made free to love, follow and serve our beautiful, wonderful Lord and Saviour. I urge the reading afresh of the book of Galatians to see in there the truth about religion and the freedom of life in the Spirit. To read how our Father is calling us out of the sterility of religion and all its ugliness. Its destructive rules, rituals and regulations. Compare that with the glory He sets before us as we yield to His love, and trust that He can be trusted, recognising His invitation to step out of the boat of security and familiarity, to walk on the waters of freedom, liberty and adventure with Jesus.

I am not wanting to hurt anyone with these words. I am not throwing rocks at anything other than that which is not of God.

What I am pursuing and pressing into, in God's name, is this – does your church 'worship' and live in true freedom and the liberty of the Spirit? Religion means we do not need God to 'show up'. We are able to do everything without Him, as it is all under control. We know what we are doing, how we are doing it, and why and when, and what the predictable outcomes will be. Usually down to the last minute.

Do You Love Me More Than These?

'Now the Lord is the Spirit, and where the Spirit of the Lord is, there is freedom' (2 Corinthians 3:17).

The New Testament outlines for us the example of the church at Corinth. When this group of believers met together, it tells us, *everyone* had something to contribute (see 1 Corinthians 14:26). In Acts the believers met together every day, in each other's homes, to worship, pray, study the scriptures and learn the teachings of the leaders and break bread. They met to eat together and enjoy each other's company. Worshipping God is never a 'spectator sport', with a 'performer' at the front and the 'audience' soaking up what is on offer and responding at appropriate times as they are told. There is nothing whatsoever in the Bible of that nature. It is not meant to be about 'professional' clergy and passive pew-fillers. We collectively constitute the *ecclesia* of God. That means for the body to be healthy, and vigorous as the Body of Christ, every person must fulfil their part. If not, the body will be sick. This is Paul's teaching from 1 Corinthians 12. Elders and deacons were appointed, not as officials, but as functioning members accepting responsibility within the local Body to help its well-being and mission. The term 'bishop' was never what it has become over the years. *'Episkopos'*, the Greek word translated as bishop is the term in Greek for an Elder, which was the Hebrew term for a leader. A Jewish Elder would have to be at least sixty years of age to be eligible for leadership. In a similar way, deacons, the translation of *'Diakonos'* in Greek, simply means a servant. We find them introduced in Acts chapter 6 where their responsibilities were to attend to the needs of the poor among the fellowship on behalf of everyone else. These are not exclusive official roles with status attached to them. They are means by which the growing body of believers continues in a healthy, wholesome way to follow Jesus, as each one washes the feet of the other.

The Pursuit of Pleasure

As in a human body, every part has its essential function to enable the body to work as it is intended. A human body functions with every part in complete unity and agreement. It works in harmony with every other part. This is the example of how the local body of believers is meant to act. It is not only 'The eye cannot say to the hand, "I don't need you!"' It is also 'so that there should be no division in the body, but that its parts should have equal concern for each other' (1 Corinthians 12: 21,25). No division, equal concern.

You cannot catch fish with broken nets.

Does church 'A' know what church 'B' is doing in the area where you live? Are church 'A' and 'B' getting together and sharing their hearts and visions? Are they looking at how best they can support and encourage each other? Are they pulling together in the same direction, with the same goals? If not, it is not a body, as bodies cannot function in any other way. Jesus is returning for a Bride, not a harem. These questions are basic to the healthy, righteous witness to what God is like and how His Body on earth is meant to function. If anyone's doctrine or theology prevent this, then love of doctrine or theology is greater than love for God and His children. True believers should have nothing of greater importance than the centrality and supremacy of God. Nothing and no one is more important than He and what is important to Him. Yes, what we believe is very important, but must never be more important than Jesus and His Body on earth. If our doctrine keeps us apart, then it is destroying God's purposes and pleasure in His people, as well as the purpose for which Jesus died.

Our unity begins in the Spirit, as Ephesians chapter 4 tells us. 'I urge you to live a life worthy of the calling you have received. Be completely humble and gentle; be patient, bearing with one another in love. Make every effort to keep the unity of the Spirit through the bond of peace' (Ephesians 4:1–3). Surely a life worthy of our calling is a life that passionately and purposefully pursues what is on God's heart. That purpose is our loving visible unity. See Psalm 133. A few verses later in Ephesians 4 we encounter the word 'until'. That particular 'until' is leading us to the reality of the 'unity in the faith and in the knowledge of the Son of God and become mature, attaining to the whole measure of the fullness of Christ' (Ephesians 4:13). However we think this unity may be realised, the chapter makes clear that our unity in the Spirit comes ahead of our unity in the faith. We have to become local bodies expressing the true unity of being one in Christ Jesus – 'speaking the truth in love, we will in all things grow up into him who is the Head, that is, Christ. From him the whole body, joined and held together by every supporting ligament, grows and builds itself up in love, as each part does its work' (Ephesians 4:15–16, NIV 1984).

Maturity has nothing to do with age or experience, necessarily. The history of the Church does not bring maturity, nor how long we have subscribed to our denomination. Maturity is growing up in God. 'I appeal to you, brothers, in the name of our Lord Jesus Christ, that all of you agree with one another so that there may be no divisions among you and that you may be perfectly united in mind and thought. [maturity] … there are quarrels among you. What I mean is this: One of you says, "I follow Paul"; another, "I follow Apollos"; another, "I follow Cephas"; still another, "I follow Christ." Is Christ divided? Was Paul crucified for you? … Brothers, I could not address you as spiritual, but as worldly – mere infants in Christ. I gave you milk, not solid food, for you were not yet ready for it. Indeed, you are still not ready. You are still worldly. For since there is jealousy and quarrelling among you, are you not worldly? Are you not acting like mere men? For when one says, "I follow Paul," and another, "I follow Apollos," are you not mere men?' (1 Corinthians 1:10–13; 3:1–4, NIV 1984). What picture emerges if we substitute the names of these great men for the plethora of denominations around us? God is telling us that for all our expertise, great Bible knowledge, slick services, beautiful buildings and all-age programmes, we are infants spiritually. We are acting as ordinary men, not Spirit-filled and Spirit- led disciples of Christ Jesus. We are immature, spiritual babies! If I am reading this teaching aright, our denominations are a testament to our immaturity. Imagine the glorious revelations yet to be revealed as we enter into maturity. The deep, hidden things of God ready to be revealed in the last days. How exciting to grasp that even now there is so much more of Him for us to experience, together.

Do you love God to the extent that everything is counted as worthless in comparison to knowing Him? Is there anything worth clinging on to if it keeps us apart from one another and the greatest fullness of life in the Spirit? I believe, in fact, I am convinced, that everything I believe in God is true. I believe things today that at one time I did not believe. I also used to believe things which I do not today. For me this has been part of the ever-exciting journey in Christ Jesus, and deeper into the heart of God. I grew up with beliefs I did not question at the time. They had been in my life from the beginning. Then fresh revelation and understanding came as the Holy Spirit led me increasingly into truth I had previously not seen.

I cannot conceive of moving away from the revelation God has given me. Nor do I believe it is necessary. All I want to be rid of is everything that is not of Him. I continue to pray, 'God, I give You permission to change my mind about anything You and I do

Do You Love Me More Than These?

not agree on.' God is never going to put His foot on my throat and force me into submission. His invitation is always to 'Come unto Me'. Some of what I am writing I find scary. I have promised Father God that I will visit and attend meetings at the church I usually pass on the way to 'my church'. This is a denomination that I struggle to honour in any way. He has whispered to me that I have to walk out what I am inviting others to do. So I have taken the plunge and walked through the doors into a fresh experience of God among a new group of relatives, brothers and sisters in Christ. Most of them live in the area I live in. Hopefully, as I get to know them, we will build a stronger expression of Jesus in our community. Worst case scenario is that I get to meet members of the Body to which I belong. At the same time I am choosing to overrule that scariness in the knowledge of His Truth that His perfect love casts out all fear (see 1 John 4:18). It is perfect love that tells us to get out of our boats of familiarity, comfort and security to walk on the turbulent waters of the unknown towards one another, secure in His love and peace.

We are all in the same battle against the powers of darkness. We are all building in cooperation with Jesus His One Ecclesia Body on earth. Every truly born again, blood-washed, redeemed child of God, however we take our place within the local believing community, is called to be working and building together in a complete 'healthy body' way to see the fulfilment of God's purposes in the earth.

We are not here to do our own thing. None of us would ever confess to such an objective, but I have seen too much over the years to naively think this does not happen. We are never here to establish a reputation, build an edifice to our own achievements. Our allegiance is completely to Jesus. He alone is the source of our life, the substance of our life, the sustainer of our life, and the satisfaction of our life. I see no room for self in this. Surely our devotion to Him supersedes our position, ambition, reputation, denomination, stream or ministry. God calling us into a unity that mirrors the relationships we see in God, is not an option reserved for visionaries or idealists. It is His heart, to be taken hold of seriously. It calls forth repentance, prayer, intercession, humility, service, and a lifestyle of foot-washing. It demands a commitment to not allow anything to block or hold up the fulfilment of this most treasured yearning of the heart of our Father God. His pleasure is seeing us as one, as He is. Who wants to give *Abba* God pleasure? Who wants to receive *Abba* God's pleasure? I know in my own experience that this is a very difficult invitation from Father God for us. There are fellowships I cannot commit myself to joining because I cannot endorse their outlook or doctrines. I have tried, but I become convicted that I am supporting stuff that is contrary to the redemptive witness of the resurrection. But I choose to encounter the family in these fellowships. I want to stay in a place where I welcome and embrace my brothers and sisters without judgement so that we may become one in reality. I choose to pray that Holy Spirit will bring revelation that will transform belief systems and practices while wanting my own heart to become increasingly sensitive to God and His desires.

The diversity which demonstrates the creative heart of God, is, I believe, seen in the imaginative ways we demonstrate our devotion to God. The skills He has gifted us with, the anointing on each of our lives, the calling to serve Him in a particular way. This is so diverse. Never boring or predictable.

Paul used the analogy of the human body. This cannot be overemphasised. I am using the analogy of a sports team. Every member of the team wears the same 'uniform' and colour. This distinguishes the team from every other. And the team never

Do You Love Me More Than These?

changes what it wears. We are always clothed in the righteousness of God. We are always robed in love. Every member of the team is skilled and equipped for the responsibilities within the team. The team work as one, for one another, with the same exclusive objective. All contribute to this one objective. The whole team is credited with success, not simply the individual who gained the success. And this is never dull or boring. The Holy Spirit is an exciting Being. Like the wind blows where it wants to, so He moves as He wills to fulfil the purposes of God in the earth. The net is not dull or boring. The net is prized for what it is able to accomplish, namely, gather a harvest of fish. The Spirit causes a stir in the community. His actions cannot go unnoticed. Being one together in Him is far more exciting than I dare to believe. And He lives in you and in me. He is able to do 'exceeding abundantly above' all we can dream or imagine according to the power at work in us (Ephesians 3:20, KJV). All we have to do is let Him, and cooperate in the joyful task.

Do you love Him more than holding on to what you have?

Do you love Him to the extent that you trust Him? Trust Him for revelation as to 'how'? Trust Him as to the 'what if's'?

Love Him to the point of maybe losing face among peers?

Love Him to the extent that you do not dismiss these words out of hand?

Will God, the Ultimate Delight, see the delight of His people delightedly releasing themselves from everything that stands against, or prevents His heart's cry, 'that all of them may be one, Father, just as you are in me and I am in you. May they also be in us so that the world may believe that you have sent me' (John 17:21)?

'I in them and you in me. May they be brought to complete unity to let the world know that you sent me and have loved them even as you have loved me' (John 17:23, NIV 1984).

The Pursuit of Pleasure

It is time for us to mend our nets. Remember Jesus' words in Matthew 12:25 that every kingdom divided against itself will fall. If anyone believes that what we see as 'church' today is what God wants, then I weep for you. If anyone believes the death of Jesus was to create the fragmented, disjointed, suspicious, often fault-finding, sometimes arrogant, frequently judgemental broken net we call 'church', then they read a different Bible to me and believe in a different god. I know there are fellowships across the land which generously live out the gospel in fragrant love and service to God and humankind. I rejoice in this. I bless this. I cry to God for more of this till this nation is fragranced by the grace and glory of God overflowing every fellowship and spilling onto the streets, into the homes, schools, businesses and centres of government. This vision burns within me as a fiery passion for the glory of God to be seen in His *ecclesia*, and to fill the whole earth. A passion for the world to know that Jesus is Lord of lords and King of kings. A passion for the Bride to eagerly, purposefully and passionately make herself ready so that she is without spot or blemish at the coming of her Bridegroom-King. The Ultimate Delight of her heart.

> Love so amazing, so divine,
> Demands my soul, my life, my all.
> ('When I Survey the Wondrous Cross', Charles Wesley, 1707–88)

And it won't even seem like a sacrifice.

My prayer is that the Holy Spirit will bring us to that place of great abandonment and joy that as one we will welcome our glorious Bridegroom-King and enter into the fullness of pleasure in Him that awaits us. For where our treasure, is that is where our hearts will be grounded.